"In *Making Time*, [barcode obscures] n-
esty into a vision [...] ve
are. This is a book [...] becoming that speaks straight to the
maker's soul."

K.J. Ramsey, therapist and author of
The Book of Common Courage

"Though *Making Time* at once inspires its reader to do as it suggests and announces its intention with delight—hey, everyone, it's MAKING time!—here is more than a self-help book about creativity. Maria Bowler has written a spiritually generous, deliciously well-researched, irreverently anti-capitalist manifesto for anyone compelled to create in an age of consumption. Bowler's creative wisdom runs deep; her social critique cuts sharply; her convictions stand firm and bold."

Rachel Lyon, author of *Fruit of the Dead* and
Self-Portrait with Boy

"Wow! *Making Time* is so wise and wonderful, so insightful and profound! I want to reread it annually. Every page contains gems of truth to help release you from productivity culture, embrace your creative identity, and live more freely. If you're caught feeling that your worth is found in your doing, if you feel a little bullied by time and to-dos, if you yearn for a life of more meaning, truth, and connection, Bowler offers the gentlest, most harmonic wake-up call. An antidote to the tyranny of productivity culture, *Making Time* can set us free to live lives that are truly worth living. I've run out of fingers and toes thinking of all the people I plan to give this book to."

Heather Lanier, assistant professor of creative writing at Rowan
University, author of *Raising a Rare Girl* and
Psalms of Unknowing

"With gentle wisdom, *Making Time* guides readers toward reclaiming a deeply buried truth about rest and being. This work of art is the salve to what ails us as a lost and imbalanced society."

Ellen Vora, MD, psychiatrist and author of
The Anatomy of Anxiety

"*Making Time* by Maria Bowler is a profound and poetic guide for anyone yearning to befriend their innate creativity. This book disarms the spiritual anguish of being trapped in cycles of achieving, performing, and producing, and lights a pathway back to the artistic capacity we each possess. Reading Bowler's wise and gentle invitations, I felt the shame and urgency of my 'doing self' give way for making again. Her writing reminds us that creative fulfillment is alive and within reach."

Amelia Knott, art psychotherapist and author of
The Art of Thriving Online

MAKING TIME

MAKING TIME

A New Vision for Crafting
a Life beyond Productivity

MARIA BOWLER

BakerBooks

a division of Baker Publishing Group
Grand Rapids, Michigan

© 2025 by Maria Bowler

Published by Baker Books
a division of Baker Publishing Group
Grand Rapids, Michigan
BakerBooks.com

Printed in the United States of America

Library of Congress Cataloging-in-Publication Data
Names: Bowler, Maria, 1985- author.
Title: Making time : a new vision for crafting a life beyond productivity / Maria
   Bowler.
Description: Grand Rapids, Michigan : Baker Books, a division of Baker Publishing
   Group, [2025] | Includes bibliographical references.
Identifiers: LCCN 2024015767 | ISBN 9781540904072 (paperback) | ISBN
   9781540904706 | ISBN 9781493449071 (ebook)
Subjects: LCSH: Time management. | Motivation (Psychology) | Self-actualization
   (Psychology)
Classification: LCC HD69.T54 B68 2025 | DDC 650.1/1—dc23/eng/20240514
LC record available at https://lccn.loc.gov/2024015767

Cover design by Lauren Smith

The author is represented by Alive Literary Agency, www.AliveLiterary.com.

Baker Publishing Group publications use paper produced from sustainable forestry practices and postconsumer waste whenever possible.

25   26   27   28   29   30   31   7   6   5   4   3   2   1

For Nate and Ingrid,
who do not need to do anything to be pure magic.

In another way, for:
The judging, tsk-tsking, punishing, "well isn't that cute,"
"just try harder" voices within me and in the world,
who mistook producing for creating.
Thank you for the inspiration.

CONTENTS

9

Contents

PART II
UNDOING
If I Am Not What I Do,
How Will I Know What to Do?

Contents

PART III
MAKING
How to Bring Your Inner World
to the Outer World

PREFACE

This is not the kind of book that will tell you what to do. I assume you're tired of other people's formulas, instructions, and hot tips anyway.

Read it then not as a user manual but rather in the same way you would read a message in a bottle washed onto the shore: just let the words land with you wherever you are.

Read it from front to back, following the journey from mere doing to making. Or open it to any page.

Who am I to instruct you anyway?

The writer of this manifesto is first and foremost someone who was once sick from the pressure to produce, though I had every social opportunity. I'm the child of the white Canadian middle class, born in the "me first" 1980s. The unspoken motto in my social sphere was "If you want it, you can make it happen if you work hard enough for it. As long as it's reasonable." Reasonable things to want included good grades, clothes from the Gap, a mortgage, and framed accomplishments to decorate the walls.

But I was also born a girl who loved to sing, a builder of cardboard castles, the first to don a cape from the dress-up pile. I had the same gift held by every child: a living imagination in which the logic of wonder makes the most sense.

Fast-forward twenty years. Picture me paralyzed from over-whelm, alone in a basement apartment with too many mice and no furniture, struggling to roll off the floor mattress (a loan from my landlord) to arrive late to work at a coffee shop serving bored tourists. Doctors called it depression. Counselors called it "over-thinking." My parents called it "Maybe you should go back to school and become a lawyer." Privately, I called it "the grayness"— a dull, ambient feeling that each day was a repeating task in which I rearranged dead objects for maximum efficiency.

From the outside, I was not producing the so-called value that society expected from someone with my privileges. I simply could not, and I felt deeply ambivalent about trying. After nearly being fired multiple times from my barista job for being generally apa-thetic, I did the only thing I knew how to do at the time: attack the problem with the mind.

All I knew at that point was this: the opposite of "the grayness" was the multicolor of making with the world around me—making beauty, making meaning, making a life. I remembered that much from my days of childhood play. With that breadcrumb, I crawled back to my hometown to finish my bachelor's in art history, study-ing photography, history, and philosophy. I found my way to a fancy Ivy League graduate school to study creativity and theories of meaning-making. For two years, I studied under Benedictine nuns to learn the mysteries of the contemplative life and how to accompany others.

This granted me the great gift of sitting across from seekers and people wondering how their inner life might feel more alive in the day-to-day. Over and over, I heard their stories of trying and failing to do enough—to meditate enough, write enough, spend time with their kids enough.

I moved to New York to rub shoulders with fancy cultural types and took my seat in a cubicle as a magazine editor in a tall build-ing in Manhattan, discussing Big Ideas. That all looks acceptable on a CV.

I went on to teach the creative process to university undergraduates as an MFA candidate in poetry and studied coaching—the inner game of outer accomplishment.

As I clawed my way out of my own pit, I set out to understand what the pressure to produce was doing to me, my clients, and my students, and how it differed from making something real, like a life that felt alive.

Then I had no choice but to stop producing. I was about to give birth as the world shut down in the spring of 2020.

You may remember that the world was beginning to freeze in response to the global pandemic. In the weeks between checkups with my ob-gyn, borders closed and best practices changed by the day. In a locked-down hospital, my husband and I celebrated baby Ingrid's entrance into the world as the nurse declared that she had a "well-shaped head." As I was wheeled out of surgery, I held her, singing, "You are my sunshine, my only sunshine."

My half-drugged self who chose that song must have known what was coming, since that was the beginning of a time filled with darkness. Night and day blurred together since my daughter didn't care for sleep. My husband worked long hours and overnights, so having any semblance of a blissful newborn cocoon was laughable. With my family living on the other side of shuttered borders and quarantines keeping friends and help at a distance, I had little human contact except this new soul. I called my own mother over and over—"I don't know what to do. I don't think I can do this." I had truly come to the end of my doing. A new way of being had to emerge.

Every day I sank into the nursing chair in the darkness as my colicky newborn daughter lay on my chest, wailing with life. There was nothing to do but be with her. There was nothing to do but be with myself. The old grayness returned with new urgency as if to say "Remember me?" as my tears fell on my baby's head. The grayness raised its eyebrows at me every evening to question what the point of all this inconvenient sitting was.

The nurses and doctors tasked to follow up with me called it postpartum blues, but I knew this was not simply a hormonal dip or just the undesirably isolating circumstances of her birth. It was a confrontation demanding an answer: "Who are you *being* when you are not out there doing? How alive can you stand to be exactly where you are, as you are?"

This baby was so terrifyingly alive. I wrote in my notebook: "The baby insists. She insists on insisting. Shushing makes screaming. She will take the warmth she wants and no warmth she does not need. She is done when she is quiet and no quiet until she is done done done. Milk, my heartbeat, and darkness."

New life starts in the dark. With nothing to do in these wee hours, I could feel my producing self hang back for long enough that memories surfaced to form a picture in my mind's eye. I could sense in my body—not just "know"—how my days studying contemplation with the nuns and creative craft with the poets and professors were showing me the same thing: what it looks like to be intimate with the creative process of life itself, not the result. The capacity to make rich meaning did not live in the artist's studio, the meditation practice, the university classroom, or a well-organized desk. Maybe everything I needed to wake up was confronting me as my pain, my *stuff*, my *problem to be solved*.

Loving attention to the process means the good, the true, and the beautiful we long for arises from whatever is unfolding now. Could it be that simple? Maybe the sparks that make the spiritual life alive, a piece of art alive, and my own plain life in this mire of isolated new motherhood feel alive all fly from that creative collision between love and reality.

That thread leads me to you and others who have also felt blocked, who know there is something more than productivity to measure the days, who long to express the truth of who they are— makers in the broadest sense of the word. When we collaborate with reality, we are makers. We are makers when we act in response to life from our true *being*, instead of merely doing. On the making path we remember we are in relationship with a living world, not just conquering things on our to-do list or molding the world to our utilitarian purposes.

Like my daughter, and much like the force of her presence I felt in those early days, we are all born makers. We are all born to make a life, after all. Yet we are conditioned to become producers, and that is where our work of unlearning begins.

We can unlearn how to "produce" a good life, good work, good art, good kids, whatever the distant prize.

As a coach, teacher, and spiritual director I have sat across from hundreds of faces as a guide, helping people unlearn roles defined by the churn of production, to build relationships to what is actually happening in themselves. Past the right schedule, past the checkboxes and gold stars, past my "best self now," to my actual self in this moment.

The more you pour in to the relationship with your natural creative process, the way you inherently make meaning with your time and effort, and the more you turn away from arbitrary checkboxes and gold stars, the more flexible and energetic your capacity for making grows.

It's no different from any other relationship; your loving attention creates intimacy, trust, and strength. I cannot "fix" my wailing baby girl, but I can learn who she is becoming. As I watch and respond to her as she is, and not as a problem to be minimized, I become a person who can respond to more of life. New colors appear on my palette.

When I was studying poetry in my MFA, we were taught to read any "I" in the poem as a hypothetical speaker, not the poet literally confessing as in a legal document. What follows are notes addressing "you," which is really a part of myself addressing another—my being speaking to your being. I trust that the "you" I speak to will find you as it needs to.

Doing, the first section, explains the insidious problem of our producer identity: how it sneakily shapes our efforts, our thinking, our relationships, our time, and how we treat the world. The next section, called Undoing, shows how to strip away the layers of doing. Finally, the Making section invites us into creative action: what it looks like to act from our deep identity as makers, not producers.

I am a student of life's ongoing process, forever and always. I offer this meditation from my deep conviction that when we forget our natural creativity, we are not well—individually or collectively.

And I am so delighted this found you.

INTRODUCTION

A great weariness haunts our days that no amount of bubble baths, life hacks, sleep solutions, nutritional supplements, or correct opinions about the news can fix.

The institutional structures we relied on to provide both security and a promise of success continue to erode before our eyes, and our collective trust in their authority crumbles with it. Those 24/7 banks, leather-bound laws, and secular and religious leaders with shiny teeth simply can't reliably tell us what to do with our lives.

These dissolving social structures leave a blank space in front of us, and our culture's habit is to fill this space with doing enough.

After all, humans are meaning-making creatures who want our time to count. How? We're not sure, but we are burdened by the sneaking suspicion that we must have something to show for our hours, our efforts, our years alive. So we buy activity trackers and read books with secrets and steps to give us clear direction, each promising that if we maximize effort, or do it the "right way," we will scratch the deeper itch. When that doesn't work, we settle for soothing ourselves. There is plenty to distract us.

But we're left with this restless set of unspoken questions. When do I get to the *after* part of the story—when do I get to coast and be who I want to be? When will I stop worrying about running out of time, money, energy, and love so I can do what I *really* want to do? (What is it that I really want to do again?)

Even those of us who have the luxury of ample time for rest find ourselves outrunning the ghost of mere doing. Did I rest well enough? Did I do chilling out right? Did I do leisure—I must never forget to be *grateful*—in a morally correct way? And why do I still feel tired after plenty of couch lounging?

This all grows from an identity problem—the hidden belief we whisper to ourselves—"I am merely what I do." When we believe that, of course we don't just *stop all our producing*, because then who would we be?

And there are so many well-meaning management strategies: time-blocking, micro habits, waking at 4:00 a.m., deliberate delegation, better boundaries, less time at work, more time at the farmer's market. If only we could get the tasks right, we could live as who we really are.

While we may have once primarily defined ourselves by our class, our religion, or our social status, we see ourselves now as producers, operating solo. Producers of "value," of content, of righteousness, of the right image, of experiences for our family—of enough, enough, enough. Enough what? It's not clear, but "it" never seems to arrive.

But of course we are not producers for some faceless boss in the sky evaluating our value, our input-output ratio—even if the aim is noble and of service to others. The point of our days was never a return on investment, as if our bodies held the same purpose as an asset in a financial portfolio.

Every spiritual and philosophical tradition worth its salt says so.

This book is an invitation to practice your inherently creative nature ahead of your impressive ability to "get stuff done," to ask "Who am I being?" before asking "How do I fix this?"

The difference I'm proposing is subtle at first, because it's not about what you do at all: doing more, less, or better. That would only reinforce our false identity as *doers first*. The difference is remembering who you already are: a maker, a human crafting meaning from your very being. *What you do* is no longer the focus, since the doing will follow naturally as you connect to who you are as your birthright.

The truth is, it is conventional for a self-help book to promise an "after" in which your life is better. After all, why would you read the book if you did not want something to look at least a little different than it did before? So I'm in a bit of a pickle because I am not offering an "after" as much as a "now" and "meantime"—a way of seeing your life as a creative process before any result, in the middle of the mess, and when your work is over. That is creative living.

Being in your life as a creative process will not free you from the challenges of the human experience—What life would that be?—but it will connect you to reality as it lives and breathes in you. This aliveness is not a reward for your production, it is simply the truth of who you are.

I'm inviting you to evaluate your time and effort *creatively*, not *productively*. As a maker, a fully alive collaborator in a vast web of creation, effort takes on a whole new meaning. When life is not a series of deliverables toward an end result, entirely new possibilities appear, as the pressures to produce lift.

Creative action is a very different animal than productivity-bound action. The results of creative action always draw out more life. The result of our productivity is simply more doing.

Compare an oak tree growing acorns that it surrenders to the ground, which creates more trees, to sending more emails from your inbox, which makes more replies you have to answer in return.

One is creative, the other "productive."

Producing is simply moving objects around the board. We will know the difference by the resulting satisfaction, the life that's made in the aftermath of creating.

To create is to cooperate with the raw materials of reality—the good, the bad, the gnarly, the extremely imperfect working

21

conditions. It is a never-ending relationship with every season of growth, including silent hours in which it appears no new life will sprout, when nothing is happening.

When there is loving attention to how the process of life unfolds, the human heart yearns to join in.

These pages are a call to the kind of action that makes whole lives and new worlds, an invitation to make your days reflect what you know to be good, true, and beautiful instead of abiding by inherited rules that perpetuate doing and death.

Feel free to rip these pages up and make your own principles with the same reckless conviction. Every time we practice a way of being beyond mere doing, we make it easier for others to practice with us.

After all, that's our job as natural makers: to play with what is possible. No need to white-knuckle your way to an abstract idea of an ideal life, you only need the presence to allow the life that wants to move through you right now.

PART I

DOING

How Productivity Has
Shaped the Way We See
Everything, for the Worse

PRODUCTION STARTS NOW

We are born with the imagination and profound capacity to *make* with life itself. This is who we are deep down.

So how did we become producers instead? How did productivity become the measure for making meaning in our lives?

The problem starts with clocks.

There was a time when time itself was a response to the sun's height and the moon's face, to birth and death, to how life bloomed and decayed by its own measure.

Your personal time simply could not be understood outside your relationship to your environment, nor could it be saved, bought, sold, or leveraged. Time was a flowing place you inhabited, not an object to manage.

After all, the dawn after the first frost is a very different kind of hour than noon on the summer solstice. The herd must graze when it needs to graze and the crops won't wait to grow.

Your interior seasons, the movements of your soul, were no different. The time to mourn came when someone died, so there was always time to mourn. That is, mourning could not become an inconvenience, standing in the way of another more important task, because there could not be a more important task. The same goes for rest and celebrating: feasting came after the harvest, which came after the growing season.

But the clocks kept getting sharper, louder, and closer to home.

In Europe, monastics left the world of agriculture and commerce to live behind walls and adopt a life of measured action within eight canonical "hours" heralded by the ringing of bells that noted the time for set prayers. The goal was to chant all 150 psalms within the week. All other monastic activities—eating, sleeping, chores, reading—were fitted in between the "hours."

Saint Benedict, the founder of the Benedictine monastic order, argued for the necessity of vigilance of time:

> If at all times the Lord looks down from heaven on the sons of men to see whether any understand and seek God, and if every day the angels assigned to us report our deeds to the Lord day and night, then, brothers, *we must be vigilant in every hour.*[1]

It might be easy to miss since we take it for granted today, but there, in one sentence, your efforts, your time, scrutinized by God, an ultimate source of meaning, are braided together as one great demand.

Timekeeping evolved from watching the stars, to water clocks, to the mechanical gears behind school bells.

In the same spirit with which your phone reports your daily steps, screen time (up 25 percent from last week), and GPS location, ever-more-accurate measurements became necessary as markers for our earthly status.

Outside the monasteries, early Protestantism nurtured a hatred of idleness and a love of time awareness. Sociologist and historian Max Weber would famously link this industriousness and the "Protestant ethic" to the need for Calvinists to display worldly prosperity as a sign of their divine election (the question of whether they were "saved" and destined for heaven, which was otherwise unknowable).[2]

Benjamin Franklin, progenitor of the productivity hack, in the late eighteenth century stretched his philosophy of advantage-seeking into the realm of time management, creating a detailed daily planner in which he assigned himself tasks and tracked his progress on acquiring new virtues.

How were early Americans to know how they were doing, in the cosmic sense, unless they were *doing* efficiently, visibly, and successfully? The question sounds familiar.

As Enlightenment-style thinking like Franklin's sought to treat our efforts in the world ever more "objectively," outside our direct experience of reality, the orderly ticking of the clock became a way to order our thoughts. And as much of the world grew disenchanted, God no longer seemed to watch the clock that called the people to worship. Instead the clock was like a god in itself—felt but unseen, ever present and impossible to refuse.

This was good for business.

In the late nineteenth century, Frederick W. Taylor, a steel industry foreman turned management consultant, looked around America's growing industrial sector and saw thousands of hours of lost productivity that could be reclaimed through a sharper focus on doing. "Of all the habits and principles which make for success in a young man," Taylor argued, "the most useful is the determination to do, and to do right, all those things which come his way each day, whether they are agreeable or disagreeable; and the ability to do this is best acquired through long practice in doggedly doing."[3]

Since turning everything into a science was the fetish of the day, this feverish talk of "doing" required a set of methods.

The result was Taylor's famous 1909 text, *The Principles of Scientific Management*. It envisions work as a series of micro tasks done in micro units of time. The scientific manager "specifies not only what is to be done but how it is to be done and the exact time allowed for doing it."[4]

Where the monks and the Calvinists used such obsessive time-vigilance for self-discipline, Taylor and his friends used it to discipline others.[5]

It was an open secret at the time that proponents of scientific management drew inspiration from the industrial model pioneered in the US South that relied on the enslavement of Black Americans.

A congressional committee hearing on scientific management in 1911 concluded that parts of the system functioned "the same as the slave driver's whip."[6]

Scientific management luminary Henry Gantt, who grew up in a family that enslaved more than sixty people, acknowledged that the system was "disliked by many men" because of its connection to slavery.[7]

Despite this, and despite a very mixed record in actually lifting productivity, Taylor and others believed it could be used to improve the running of "all social activities," and the system spread far and wide.[8]

What was good for business must be good for everyone.

Not only was it adopted at Ford Motor and in Soviet five-year plans, it was also imposed upon pastors in American Protestantism. Ministers were often expected to become "efficiency experts" and each church made into a "General Efficiency Board for the Kingdom of God."[9]

When they dragged the notion of scientifically managing time into the office, "efficiencies" were not only physical and cognitive but emotional as well.

As C. Wright Mills put it in the 1950s, "When white-collar people get jobs, they sell not only their time and energy but their personalities as well."[10] This led to annoyingly human complaints about both physical and mental ailments, including muscle strain, irritability, digestive trouble, and depression.[11]

And that was not good for business.

Partially in response to this, the Austrian-American professor Peter Drucker's 1954 work, *The Practice of Management*, created a broader, more white-collar-friendly theory of management. He would popularize the term "knowledge worker" and "information society" and urge more respect for the value of employees.[12]

This "respect" gave workers the supposed freedom to be their own time manager. Where Taylor drew a clear line between workers and management (the workers were the doers, the managers were the deciders and evaluators), now you are probably both—in every area of life.

In addition to your actual job descriptions, paid or unpaid, you must decide what it is to do—since you swim in endless options and opinions about the one best way. We are now all project managers, all the time.[13]

And worse, if your work is less tangible than shoveling iron, you have to come up with elaborate ways to count your efforts under the clock. Unless you use your hands to make or fix things (and fewer and fewer jobs give us such touchable results), your work feels ephemeral.

Such are the weather conditions in the land of productivity. The time you manage is clock time, which counts every minute as a unit from which to extract the most value for an invisible judge, a unit of debt owed to an invisible bank. This leaves the sticky question "What happened today? Did I do anything valuable? Does this even matter?" As the accounting historian H. Thomas Johnson put it, "What you don't (or can't) measure is lost."[14]

So you are earnestly debating with yourself about the best uses of time: whether weekends are best spent with family, whether morning or evening is better for cardio, or whether it's selfish to write poetry instead of fighting climate change.

Each option points to the same clock under which time is for using. In this poisonous producer's life, the hours will never be enough as the existential question looms: Did I make today *count* by an invisible measure?

Even as we live in the land of productivity, it's time to remember who we really are.

THE OTHER PATH

Your sense that the way you're working is not working means you are awakening from the spell of the producer.

Do not rid yourself of that nagging hunger for more aliveness, because you would not feel it if you could not be fed. It is, as Martha Graham said to Agnes de Mille, the artist's "queer, divine dissatisfaction, a blessed unrest" to keep creating. While Graham thought this "divine dissatisfaction" was what makes the artist "more alive than the others,"[1] I'm pushing the premise a step further to insist that it belongs to everyone, that there are no "the others."

Whether you have ever thought of yourself as "a creative," a noun that didn't exist until recently, the ambient restlessness that has you reading this book is the same impulse that leads to all acts of beauty, truth, and goodness: your sneaking suspicion that more life is available here.

A maker is someone who cooperates with reality to draw out more life: someone who receives the stuff around them not as objects to extract value from, but as an unfolding world to playfully connect with. You're a maker as you turn a terrible date into a funny story you'll tell for years, broker peace between arguing friends, invent sneaky ways to hide all the power cords in your living room, and listen to someone long enough that they lean back in their chair, breathing deeply as they have been heard. You mend, whether it's wool socks or past mistakes. You disturb stagnant places, draining standing water so it can flow again or speaking up to city council. You invent. You imagine. You are on the maker's path, which is a very different way of being than the conveyer belt of production. The path of making says "Yes, I exist" to the heights and depths of your humanity, from your dreamiest imagination to your most shadowed thoughts and deeds.

All the inefficiencies that get in the way are not obstacles to eliminate but a maker's material to work with. Not good, not evil, simply reality that beckons your attention.

A maker does not simply do more but makes more meaning from every act, which your soul cannot help but do when you let it.

You can fail to follow a five-step plan, but you cannot fail to be a maker, because your life is making *you* all the time. You can only forget that, or drag your heels.

There is nothing more to do, and you're already doing it. You can't fail to make because making is who you are. You can only temporarily forget, putting on production's clothes.

If that's true, your only "task" is saying yes to conscious collaboration, turning every part of the process into a live conversation.

For your cooperation, you are not given a different set of to-dos but a clear pair of eyes with which to see how beauty, truth, and goodness are always giving themselves form, even now. In your fluorescent-lit office. On your couch. Through the pings on your phone.

MERE DOING

When you're a producer, as we have all been trained to be, you can't consciously act as much as *do*. Doing more, or if that doesn't work, doing *differently*, is the only key to unlocking all the doors that appear before you.

You do because *not* to do conjures a ghost with many names: the Threat of Unemployment, Moral Condemnation for Being a Lazy Loser, the Sound of Your Own Thoughts.

The exact sound and shape of the ghost will shift throughout the day, some days parroting your cruelest teacher's voice, on other days piping up to remind you of apocalyptic headlines or eviction notices.

But the main quality of all this doing is how temporary it is; it can only keep the ghost outside the door of your room until you stop. If you must stop, worrying about what you're not doing is the only other acceptable offering.

I call this kind of action "mere doing," as opposed to taking meaningful action. *Mere* means "nothing more, nothing less," because even the best productivity strategy can make you nothing more or nothing less than exactly who you have been before—yet the sun sets and rises and you are one day older.

Perhaps you will swap your jeans for well-tailored silk trousers, or admire the gleaming countertop that replaced the old laminate, but nothing has *grown* nor has any life decayed as it must. The same you, with the same understanding, is only wrapped in a new slick cover to ensure you keep working. At its best, mere doing might give you a pretty life, but it won't give you a fuller one.

You know this already. There's an itch that no doing can scratch.

Mere doing is always demanding you answer the question "What do I do about *that*?"—where *that* is a feeling or an unanswerable question such as "What is my soul's purpose?" or "My kid isn't sharing with me about their day, and I'm uncomfortable." You can feel the way it forces you to react to life as a harm-reduction strategy instead of a creative act.

You can only do or not do.

Mere doing is a desire to exert completion and control. It's in the way our hands twitch to fix as we watch a child build a wobbly tower from blocks instead of simply watching.

This "doing" takes no vacations. It's inescapable in this part of the world, sending its appeals straight to the brain's survival instinct. The late capitalist version adds in a constant awareness of the surveillance devices in our pockets, plus the threat of joblessness, plus the threat of the end of civilization.

If it's a kind of disease, you did not generate it from a uniquely messed-up mind. You do not get it *only* from your job, your parents, your religion, or your kids. It is passed among all of us like oxygen. It does not heal itself naturally when you retire. Every single time your parents promised that if you ate your broccoli, you could go play, you learned that doing the thing was the ticket to freedom. The apparent urgency in every job description, every bullet point in a For Dummies book, every product recommendation, every advice column with a script for how to respond to a troubled friend, traffics in mere doing. It's not your fault.

"And what will you do with that degree?"

"So are you going to dump him?"

"What did you get up to this weekend?"

"How will you fix that?"

Just hand in the assignment. Just take out the garbage. Just complete the deliverables. Just make your kid stop crying. Then you can have the ideal life, or at least an okay one. Then you can belong.

The pressure to merely *do* is most clear when you're faced with the worthiest, most beautiful tasks—the things you really *want* to do: growing peonies to hide the old fence, telling your boss the truth as you see it, hosting a feast for your two closest neighbors, declining to join yet another committee, starting a club, singing Anita Baker at your local open mic, writing the great Canadian novel.

Those actions don't bend to the force of mere doing so easily. They are the actions that speak to the maker in you. This is the reason you hesitate before those things you really want to do.

You merely *do* out of habit, anxiety, and the compulsion to avoid the empty space your productivity can never fill. As Nietzsche put it, "Haste is universal because everyone is in flight from himself."[1]

But you are not a producer, you are a maker. One of Hannah Arendt's insights in *The Human Condition* is that we develop the roots of our identities through our interaction with the *stuff* of the world, in relationship to the durable things we and others make. "The things of the world have the function of stabilizing human life," Arendt writes.[2]

Our capacity to create things also creates our identities. As producers, we see the world as a warehouse for dead objects. As makers, our relationship to the world is defined by our understanding that it is like us: deeply alive.

This is in contrast to the part of us that labors, an activity which Arendt sees as much less permanent and geared primarily toward survival, as well as in contrast to the part of us dedicated to action or *praxis*, the basic ingredient of human togetherness and politics, the way we reach out directly into the world and make decisions with others, sharing who we are with them.

34

We contain all of this, and despite the emphasis on distinguishing between the parts, the threads between them are important.

A maker's actions are creative moves that declare specific statements about what it is to be human. Whether you are making yourself tea, a spreadsheet, or a political speech, the quality of action is one of an intimate relationship between the maker and the world—as opposed to doing, where you are acting on it and running from it.

DOING SURVIVAL

You may allow yourself to release the pressure to produce your way through life in theory, but perhaps it seems naive to take it too far. Part of you believes the survival of what really matters depends on it.

If you've lived long enough, you have produced a lot of your success thus far. It makes sense that you would want to keep forcing yourself to produce as an option, just in case.

But you must go to the heart of your fear of what would happen if you truly stopped being the producer. If you dropped all the balls you're keeping in the air and they all fell, who would you be? What would your arms be doing? I asked an artist and teacher what she would do if her jobs disappeared tomorrow. After a pause, she said, "After panicking, I might see who I am. I might hear myself. Then I'd look for another job."

You will never feel free within the limits of your time, money, and the goodwill of others until you make peace with the fact that there will come a day when the limits win.

We will all ultimately lose the survival game, because even the most prolific among us will die. The role of a maker is to embrace death on purpose so you don't need to spend your energy avoiding the small deaths that come every day: the meeting that goes nowhere, the friendship drifting away, the plans canceled due to rain, the last bite of Christmas dinner.

Otherwise, what is the end of all you're doing? Will you let there be an end at all?

Your productivity lands you in a civil war with your own finitude. A producer is defined by this inner war with scarcity, the limits of time and the decay of our most shining efforts. This is one of many unwinnable wars the producer wages with reality itself as they use stoplights to respond to texts and tell themselves they "shouldn't" be sick.

The paradox is that your arguments with how limited your time and energy are keep you feeling bound by them.

The world cannot be full of life for a producer when they are focused on avoiding death. We see the avoidance not only in our culture's neuroticism about literal death, which we keep far away in hospitals and out of our conversation with euphemisms, but also in microcosms of death: deep sleep, "wasted" time, the end of a favorite status quo.

The animal in your humanity wants to stay alive. This is the part of you that gets a thrill from those acts of maintenance and upkeep that make you feel like you're cheating death just a little. When you cleaned out your garage, emptied the gutters, sealed all the food around your campsite to keep the grizzly bears at bay.

And then there is the manufactured scarcity that has us pay to belong on this planet, the inherited declarations that there is just not enough for everyone as "winner takes all." The producer takes this at face value because on some level they must in order to keep up, since despite being manufactured, the scarcity knocks on our doors and pops up in our inboxes. It is very understandable that managing scarcity becomes a mental obsession. And then sneakily, slowly, as we become "responsible adults," the obsession itself does us harm, like an unlucky charm we keep thumbing in our pockets.

A producer is very busy trying not to run out of countable things—minutes, monies, means. A producer must simply keep going, without creative choices about what to do until he has a contingency plan for avoiding his worst-case scenario. He can't ask out his crush without convincing himself they won't say no—or that he doesn't even care if they do because there's another date on the way.

Fearing the worst-case scenario happens in the smallest ways, so quickly that we producers don't even notice. So notice: What would happen if you didn't host Thanksgiving this year? What would happen if you declined the project? What would happen if you spent hundreds of dollars on a new instrument and spent years learning how to play it?

Imagine all possible failures for each of them. See what illusions of necessity dissolve. It may be frightening at first, but you'll notice the obsession with avoiding loss will lose some of its heat.

What would happen if you truly ran out of money, whatever that means to you, and found yourself at the mercy of strangers? Take your imagination further. What exists beyond what you're avoiding?

Use the same imagination that has been trained to anticipate threats in the abstract and train it to go deeper until you can see in grimy detail whatever the "worst" is.

The way to stop being trapped by lack is to embrace it: your lack of time, breath, and motivation. To see the way that all things are collaborating creatively for abundant life, stop arguing with all the edges.

A landscape artist often uses a paper viewfinder, a small make-shift frame she places before her eyes to help her see possible compositions in nature. She cannot paint the whole world at once, and does not try.

Hold the limits before your eyes like a frame.

DOING ENOUGH

Productivity doesn't make any sense without a tantalizing promise: at some magical point, you can do enough.

Enough action that can keep the bank from foreclosing, the profits from falling, the winds from blowing, the fears from descending. The "enough" cannot be named too explicitly because that would break the illusion that it exists somewhere "out there."

The physical wellness industry promises a state of "balance" you'll prove with a flexible body and a calm mind, smooth skin ("How does she do it?"), linen dresses, and an eerily soothing voice.

The emotional wellness industry suggests you might get somewhere where you purge old patterns and hold the right boundaries so your mom never triggers you. *Finally*, a holiday at your folks' place where everyone smiles with their eyes and no one slams a door or gossips in the car on the way home.

And all that is possible. Of course it could happen—anything wonderful can happen, until the next minute when a new incompleteness arrives: the mood changes, you get a new email, you get sick, or your boss calls you complaining. From the lens of *doing*, that's when you get a new problem to solve.

In the meantime, you trudge along, mired in feelings of not-yet, diverted by side quests selling you one new proprietary process after another to *finally* arrive at "enough."

As a producer, you must fundamentally disapprove of your current status and location to get "there"—the state called "enough." Just like the concept of darkness only makes sense if there's such a thing as light, the concept of enough doesn't exist without its silent opposite: not enough. The quest to do enough demands that the producer do, do, do in the chronic state of not enough—living under the constant refrain "not quite there"—until you reach an arbitrary point that vanishes the moment you arrive.

The experience reminds me of an ill-fated expedition led by Donald MacMillan one hundred years ago. He had heard of a distant, frozen island in the Arctic spotted by another explorer, Robert E. Peary, who dubbed it Crocker Land (after one of his financial backers, naturally). MacMillan was so excited to be the first to get there and solve what he called "the world's last geographical problem," he told reporters that the land's "boundaries and extent can only be guessed at, but I am certain that strange animals will be found there, and I hope to discover a new race of men."[1] And aren't we certain that we'll find wonderful things when we arrive at *enough*?

MacMillan and his expedition party had climbed glaciers, suffered frostbite, and sledded over dangerous sea ice when he saw it—or he thought he did. "Great heavens! What a land!" MacMillan wrote. "Hills, valleys, snow-capped peaks extending through at least one hundred and twenty degrees of the horizon."[2]

His Inuit guide, Piugaattog, knew better; it was a mirage, a "poo-jok."[3] This "land" was an atmospheric illusion that appears when light bends as it passes through layers of air at varying temperatures. As convincing as it appeared, Crocker Land was a trick of perception meeting ambition.

So is the spot on the fantasy map called Enough. As you trudge through ice to get there, holding your breath against the wind, you'll have to do the same thing tomorrow and the next day.

Of course, there's nothing wrong with aiming for a target beyond reach. You might love the thrill of believing that there is no *there*, there is only *better*. In the same way a child is drawn to the top of the play structure, maybe you love challenge. There is real enjoyment in testing your limits, in competing for fun like a tiger cub playing with her siblings, in running the half marathon or plunging into cold water. But there is a vast difference between the challenge of a game where you delight in the expansion of your experience *now* versus the tease of a promised joy, or even just relief, that only comes "someday."

How many industries would crash if they never invented reasons why we are not enough? "Dandruff" was invented by advertisers as a new way to be embarrassed. They linked it to poor personal hygiene to sell their anti-dandruff shampoos as the welcome solution to this manufactured problem.

The requirement to *do* at all costs convinces you that you are uniquely broken—but not if you would complete the following steps. Mere doing will then come up with the exact calculus of mutually incompatible demands to keep you improving, not growing.

Be calm but don't get pushed around. Stay disciplined but don't be rigid. Be sensitive and aware but don't need anything. Be unique but not weird. Live in the house everyone else wants, but be true to yourself!

While you try to sleep, visions of The Time You Said the Wrong Thing will dance behind your eyelids. Remember when you screwed up? You really dropped the ball on that one. Make sure you do something different next time.

You wonder if you've done enough. Yet through it all, your maker self is unbothered. It is patient at every heavy step through the snow.

DOING MIDDLE MANAGEMENT

The working conditions are poor inside most of us.

When in production mode, we scrutinize ourselves as the doer of actions. And yet when we report for duty each day, we do not arrive as a singular person.

We show up to work with many little selves and agendas. We are born "multiple," says Richard Schwartz, who developed the Internal Family Systems model of psychological treatment.[1] In the words of Pablo Neruda, "I shall speak, not of self, but of geography."[2]

Chief among the producer's voices is an inner middle manager.

This middle manager has a very stressful job. They must monitor countable actions and predict their outcomes. They must rouse lazy employees from bed. They are responsible for everything that gets done, yet do not possess any actual authority to change the rules.

They believe they need to make the decisions with no backup, no support, and deeply resentful employees. That is the interior office culture of a frustrated tyrant.

In an actual corporate environment, you can follow through on your threats to fire people, but you can't force your inner selves to work or stop existing.

First, you experience your inner middle manager as disappointed or temporarily satisfied. But when you get to know what the inner middle manager really wants, you see that they are so very afraid of the wheels falling off.

When I talk to a maker in the throes of resistance, they come to me presenting a form of stuckness. They want to be *there*, but they are *here*. They speak in the voice of the middle manager: "I just can't get myself motivated," as if the self is a gaggle of slacking employees.

Riding herd on all your doing, your inner middle manager believes they are being watched by security cameras at some faceless corporate headquarters. Their job depends on managing employees. They have no confidence in themselves or authority to change the labor process, which they take at face value. The inner middle manager is responsible for everything and has power over nothing.

He has to make the schedules, then remake them when the other employees within you don't show up. He resents the pressure and takes it out on your poorest performing parts. He tries to give pep talks that ring hollow, because he does not have the trust of the rest of you. He has heard this quarter will be "the best quarter ever" and tries to believe it.

He cannot quit.

A maker gives a wry smile to the corporate framework of the self, the one that thinks it must be managed and mitigated. From that place, they gently take the clipboard from the middle manager's hands, saying, "You don't have to do this alone."

A maker knows that the middle manager is very afraid to receive a punishing memo from a distant CEO he's never met. A maker reminds him, "Thank you for trying so hard to hold my life together. I see all the mental effort that it takes to think about everything that can run out, then try to get back on track after interruptions. You don't know how these scattered pieces will hold together without your white knuckles around them. You have been working until you collapse, and you can lie down now."

A maker sees, despite the middle manager's insistence that there is only one way to "manage" a life, that wisdom will come from elsewhere.

A maker trusts more of the self, the world, and the process.

She is witness to the inner middle manager—his schedules, punishments, pep talks, petty theories.

She knows it is a tough job answering to the invisible boss in the sky and the real-life boss in the corner office.

She thanks him for his work and says he has earned a vacation.

DOING FREE TIME

I started my undergraduate writing class with a freewriting assignment inspired by Julia Cameron's famous "morning pages" from her book *The Artist's Way*: write three pages of stream-of-consciousness thoughts. The only rule was to keep your hand moving without stopping to fix, think, or edit.

I was grateful when a brave student asked, "What is the point?" "There is no point," I replied. "That is the point. There is nothing to get done except allow your thoughts on the page, even and especially when they don't make any sense." Allowing anything and everything in the students' minds to simply be on the page without interference *did* serve a sideways purpose: their eyes would light up, their shoulders would drop. They were learning to simply *be* while in motion: the opposite of the tight grip they had learned to write and work with.

The blank page is like open time on our calendars. As producers, we are tempted to fill it trying to get somewhere.

You itch for more flexibility, then find yourself restless and anxious with too much free time to fill with something. No matter how much freedom of movement you have in your schedule, there is something in you that feels deeply bound. Open time is a problem in the land of production.

All the calendaring systems insist that the problem lies in *when* you do all your tasks. If you could figure out the "whens," you could coast to your desired destination. A producer gives themselves this much freedom: "I don't care *when* you do it, but you must *do* eventually."

Then all manner of calendar-crowding tasks arrive, and keep arriving week after week, year after year, and you are nowhere to be found. You are still metaphorically hidden under the couch because time remains a problem to solve.

The problem is most obvious when the action you're waiting to take is personal, beloved, and life-giving—the art project, the date, the long call with a friend.

"It's only an hour until bed," you say. "There is no point. It won't be enough time."

A producer doesn't know what to do with open time because it is unnatural to look at one's actions as interchangeable tasks you can rearrange on a board with the same weight and importance.

The convenient idea that you *could* do so crashes on the rocks of who you really are. It feels *untrue* that a leisurely phone call with a friend (task 1) and submitting your taxes (task 2) could be weighed on the same scale, the one production land measures as Value Added/Risk Mitigated.

You think you want the freedom of more time, but even more you want freedom from your *relationship* with your tasks. A producer is always running out of time, because there is only one kind of time for the producer: time to do or not do.

The Eisenhower Matrix, a popular productivity tool, asks you to classify your tasks as urgent or nonurgent, and important or not important. The producer blends the urgent and important out of habit, even if she knows that the latest email is not important in the cosmic sense.

Without urgency, there is no guidance for a producer. When you remove all the urgency, you see how much direction it gave you, how it created momentum for you.

Yet even the word *important* can be co-opted by the productive mind to pull us back into production land. As producers we are not sure that we are important enough to simply exist, so let's put that word aside for now as well.

A maker sits at the intersection of time and eternity. From the writings of the ancient Greek philosopher Heraclitus: "Time is a game played beautifully by children."[1] A maker respects time enough to play in it.

Faced with open time, a maker's mind can ask, What is alive in me right now? What might make this situation come more alive? Even more, what is already alive around me now that draws my attention?

Notice that your answers get more specific and flexible than "What should I do?" You could just as easily say "a nap" as "rearrange the entire garage." For a maker, watching the bird perch on the maple tree and sending a strongly worded petition are equally beautiful acts.

Notice that feeling alive and feeling good have a new relationship. Notice how rest and regenerative action are equally available. For a maker, open time is no longer a problem to solve but a place where play and work flow in and out.

DOING DEEP EFFORT

Doing anything meaningful will require deep effort from us; there's no escaping it. Arguing with the reality of effort would be like debating gravity; no living being *becomes* without it. Seeds have to break open and push through soil to find sunlight. Every living thing needs resistance to grow. Our muscles atrophy for lack of use. We will need, maybe even desire, to test what we're made of on a given day. Effort itself is neutral—not inherently good or moral, no matter how much the producer mindset is convinced that it is. The meaning and power of our effort changes based on the way we relate to it.

For example, grinding away with force toward burnout is an awful sight to behold. Yet there can be something glorious about seeing living things give everything in them just because they can. The difference lies in what we make our deep effort mean.

Giving it all is part of your being—the way an Olympic swimmer's gleaming arms speed through the surface of the water, or a dog gleefully barrels through a field to pant happily under a tree.

The hustle of a producer is very different from the deep effort of a maker. While it's understandable that we would find ourselves trying to outwork our anxiety, an ethos of hustling will backfire in the end by reinforcing how *necessary* it is to get anything done, or else. At its root, hustling is the effort to earn our unearnable birthright: the right to live and become. It is always our attempt to outrun an unacceptable outcome instead of move toward more life.

Even as it has you speeding up, hustling manifests as hiding and procrastination in equal measure. This is the flip side of the same hustling coin: the belief that action will make or break who you are. If that's true, it's best to wait until the doing is perfect, and if it isn't, all is lost.

The public face of hustle is the glossy promise that if you can force more action into less time to wring more market value from a life disconnected from its real values, you'll feel satisfied.

The pressure has you hide this belief, even from yourself. You may be ashamed that you're forcing yourself into action, so you pretend it's just part of the game. The belief behind this quiet scramble is my actions determine my results, which prove my worth.

A producer will mistake hustle for deep effort. They only see unwinnable races held by the market, by their employers or their internal jailers. You can spot an unwinnable race by how much it involves running from a hypothetical pain.

Action done out of fear is hustle. Waiting out of fear is secret hustle.

When we believe that we are alone in our efforts, which are doomed to fail without our tight grip on making it happen (or as the title of a self-help book from the nineties put it, *If It Is to Be, It's Up to Me*),[1] of course we are going to hustle. Without our vigilance, we tell ourselves, we will be left alone with chaos.

But a maker trusts deep effort instead. Creating, the deepest kind of effort we can give, asks for our participation, not control. Results happen *through* us, not because of us. This means that the desired outcome is already there, waiting for us. The end result we imagine has already been created; we just can't see it yet.

For a maker, deep effort is fun when you believe you have already created the result you want; it's only temporarily invisible.

If that sounds fantastical, that idea has some history to it: the word *create* has ancient origins, with Sanskrit and Latin roots related to reproduction and the generating of new life. In the Middle Ages, the verb *create* itself appeared, from the past participle of the Latin verb *creare*. It was associated with already-completed acts of making, especially those performed by God.

Among the Oxford English Dictionary's list of early uses are quotes from Chaucer and the poet John Lydgate, saying things like "Al be it so that god hath creat alle thynges in right ordre"[2] and "[planets were] Eternally yformed and creat."[3]

When people started using the word to describe everyday human actions, "creating" retained its sense of already-completedness. That suggests we are not solo operators forcing stuff to happen.

When you create, your deep effort brings something that already exists in some mysterious way into form. It's more like cooperation than solo invention.

The life-giving and reproductive connotations here are no accident either.

You can think of participating in deep effort like the birthing process; once the contractions start, it's undeniable that the baby is here and on its way into your arms. The baby is not a mere idea that the birthing process makes "real." How the labor feels, how much support there is, how much pushing and resting in between contractions—those are up to the parent. But that baby is present in the birth canal.

While deep effort doesn't promise the ride will be easy, it will have a flow of its own, and the result will come, if the maker allows it.

LAZINESS IS MADE UP

You are not lazy; you are working very hard to resist a seemingly inconvenient part of your humanity. You are using both hands and all your body weight to keep it out of your awareness. You have been doing it so long that you don't even notice how heavy it is. That is what is tiring you.

Every instance of "laziness" directly connects to another thing that you are highly diligent and vigilant about.

Laziness has become a moral issue because it's useful to gain compliance if *not doing* is a character defect. Practically, groups of people living together don't work very well when there's a lot of laundry to do and fish to catch but only a handful are willing to do it. It causes resentment and chaos.

Without the resources to be curious about why some people seem to sit on the sidelines, it's simply easier to call it *idleness*, *sloth*, *entitlement*, or *laziness*. It's easier to make it a moral failing, a character defect, so as to shame people and keep them in line.

But I have never met a truly lazy person.

I worked with a librarian who referred to himself as lazy in our first call. "I would love to pray and meditate more, but I think I'm just too lazy to have the kind of practice real spiritual people have." His evidence of lazy behavior was reading graphic novels, scrolling on his phone, and a list of attempted habits that could never quite stick. When he was not telling me how unmotivated he was, he was describing his struggles at work.

He could see how much better managed the place could be, how his colleagues were frustrated, how the system could be less bureaucratic and more open to the community. His voice tightened and grew sharp when describing what he saw; it was clear this man cared deeply about the role of libraries in his city. "I just don't want to get fired or quit," he said with a sigh. All the mental effort he was putting into not losing or quitting his job, he dismissed entirely. This was a deeply passionate man who was spending so much energy resisting himself and his surroundings that he was exhausted, calling it laziness.

Gently, over a month or two, the librarian became willing to let go of his lazy label, both for himself and for his colleagues. Once he did, he began to see how much energy lived in his body that he'd only labeled as anger and frustration. Now that he could feel his natural life force, he could actually decide what to do about it.

From there, he saw what was within and outside of his control. He stopped people-pleasing his colleagues and taking on busywork he knew would not make a dent in his goals to run more diverse programs at work. He asked for, and received, the green light to run a program that had been on the back burner of his mind for years. He asked for help from, instead of silently resenting, his colleagues. He stopped taking his work home with him and found time for the spiritual practices he was "too lazy" to do.

This maker's story shows more than a tweak in motivation; it was a revolution against the cruelty of mislabeling. He didn't conquer laziness; he unmasked it. This man was not battling apathy but untangling his true desire and duty. It's a knot many of us know too well, yet often name it laziness.

This shift asks for more than a change of pace—it asks for a shift in identity. Otherwise, it's like mistaking a sleeping lion for a boulder—both might seem still, but one has far more potential for action (and, admittedly, a little more risk).

What you dismiss as laziness might actually be a deep, vigilant commitment to something you haven't yet acknowledged or acted upon. You might just be one honest reckoning away from turning apparent apathy into more life.

DREAD AND DOING

A creeping sense of dread keeps us very busy. While it's not a feeling we tend to discuss openly, it's a powerful engine for frantic action.

It doesn't need to be dramatic; quiet dread happens every day. When you see the tires wear down, the hole in your sock, the lettuce going brown before you eat it once again.

Sigh quietly. Push away the thought. Resolve that this week will be different.

It is the dread of aging that has me maxing out my credit card on expensive skin creams when I see my sagging cheeks in the mirror. I meet the thought of my growing old, my finitude, with fear and resistance, then become fixated on loss prevention.

It's like the "doomsday prepper" lifestyle, stoked by rugged-individualist conspiracies, peddling the fantasy that if you prepare well enough, impending social collapse will spare your tiny castle and you'll be safe.

Safe for what? To do what? That's never discussed. Yet there is a significant corner of the internet dedicated to best practices, comparing the best sites for your homestead and debating the most likely catastrophes. Emergency preparedness is a multibillion-dollar industry.

Doom is not simple fear or even despair; it's a potent cocktail of fatalism and resistance to that fate.

We have a culture without a profound language for safety, belonging, meaning, that goes beyond our little plot of land, our apartment, our own bodies. We are freaked out. We don't have much to say to catastrophe, or tragedy, or death. So we ignore it or we resist it and stay in Dread.

The world has ended many times. In Europe and Asia in the 530s, volcanic eruptions and a subsequent "mysterious fog" wrapped the world in darkness for eighteen months. In 1347, a new wave of the bubonic plague reached Europe, Asia, and North Africa with apocalyptic results. "So many died that all believed that it was the end of the world," according to Italian chronicler Agnolo di Tura.[1] In 1815, Mount Tambora in the Indonesian archipelago exploded, sending clouds of gases and ten billion tonnes of volcanic rock and ash into the atmosphere. The result was a volcanic winter that embraced the planet. 1816 became known as the Year Without a Summer, while English poet Coleridge called it "end of the world weather."[2]

When the ground underneath our feet shifts without our permission, as it will in vast and tiny ways, it's very tempting to fall into doom. We get to feel helpless and busy at the same time. A brewing sense of doom leads to doing that goes nowhere. When we are fixated on total defeat—whether we feel destined to repeat the past or meet a disastrous end—we doom ourselves to frantic action that keeps us exactly as we are.

In Stanley Kubrick's film *Dr. Strangelove*, an unstable US general initiates a nuclear strike against the Soviet Union, leading to an escalating doomsday scenario that careens out of control.

While the actual implementation of a universal doomsday machine hasn't happened, the theoretical underpinning of mutually assured destruction (MAD) was very real. Both the United States and the Soviet Union embraced MAD as a cornerstone of their nuclear strategies during the 1960s and '70s. Under this doctrine, the vast nuclear arsenals possessed by each nation ensured that launching a first-strike attack would leave them open to a devastating counteroffensive.

The power of these "doomsday devices" lives in their irreversibility—once they are triggered, nothing can stop them.

As Mark Fisher put it, "It's easier to imagine the end of the world than the end of capitalism."[3] Put another way, the land of productivity proposes the cataclysmic end of all we know—life will end if this doesn't happen—before admitting there are alternative ways we can feel complete. The dread is not so much about death but about living with the loss of the perfect thing to do.

While dread might make you productive for a while, it's deeply uncreative. Fatalism makes for a sorry muse. When we act busy to run from what we fear, our focus turns inward. The result is short-term relief and long-term emptiness. We fill our calendars with stopgap measures, temporary diversions that keep us from facing the underlying issues that keep us from living fully in the first place.

Still, we can act for two reasons: to create more life on our quaking earth, or to escape what we fear.

At its core, creating to bring more life into the world is an act of affirmation. If a teacher designs the curriculum to avoid looking bad in front of the classroom, her students might simply pass the tests, or not. If the same teacher crafts lessons to light up curiosity and understanding, her efforts multiply in the minds of her students long past the school bell.

DOING REST

On the floor of a breathwork class with a sleeping mask over my eyes, I listened to the throbbing techno beat overlayed with an ethereal flute.

"Repeat after me," intoned the instructor wearing a fetching coordinating set of athleisure. "I deserve to rest."

Thirty of us replied, "I deserve to rest."

"Louder!" she encouraged us. "I deserve to care for myself!"

We shouted, "I DESERVE TO CARE FOR MYSELF!"

Why did this feel like an argument? I wondered.

The land of capitalist production is always making sneaky compromises with the forces that resist it so that it can keep producing onward, if with a rebrand. When "hustle" stopped being a convincing path to success, the market had to find ways of incorporating antihustle. Suddenly personal growth leaders were proclaiming that rest is productive. In the Google Books database, instances of the term "self-care" roughly doubled between 2010 and 2019.

Rest is not productive; it's regenerative. It's part of the creative cycle of life, not an unavoidable detour on the way to getting your work done.

How many times have you collapsed on the couch after a stressful day to "rest," only to go to bed just as agitated? You've heard all the detailed advice to relax more, set boundaries on your work, and adopt self-care routines.

But your nervous system is primed to fight, still running with vigilance. Your mind is still trying actively to solve a problem, any problem. As producers, rest is another thing to do.

That's why you can "do rest," give up every task that stresses you out, and have no more spark of life than you did before. You can do all the recommended self-care, which often means buying something, and remain completely the same. This imitation rest is just productivity wearing a hydrating face mask.

Market-driven models of work have no understanding of the inner life. Your shadowy impulses, human desires, and sharp memories are aliens within the system. In this mode, rest is expected to be as smooth and frictionless as flashing your priority pass on your way to a private airport lounge. But unless we've practiced, real rest often feels awkward, at best.

To really rest, you need to give up the imperative to be good at resting. This means facing the swirling vortex around the wound of "not enough."

Real rest doesn't argue with that wound. It doesn't say, "I *deserve* to rest" because that suggests you *could* be undeserving of the state that belongs to every part of nature.

Real rest is mentally releasing the need to solve a problem, including an emotion. If you're angry, real rest says, "It's fine to be mad. I don't have to stop this anger from being here, nor do I need to stoke it or justify it." Imagine hands releasing a fist. Real rest lets your hands fall open and watches whatever you're holding slip through your fingers to the ground.

Your producer self will steal rest as a reward for what you have earned, like a mouse finally biting into cheese after winding its way through the maze. At best, it gives you temporary relief. But relief is just an absence of pain while you're still thinking about pain. In the same way, the producer just "stops working" while continuing to think about work.

The industrial model only acknowledges rest when it's obvious that you've reached a point of diminishing returns or you simply can't go on anymore. A factory reluctantly incorporates rest when faced with striking workers, or when it stops being efficient. The producer has internalized this reluctance and only allows themselves to rest if they have to give up.

When you refuse for a long time, rest has a way of sneaking in in the form of giving up.

You are a field that doesn't simply need a seasonal break from its usual crop, but one that needs nourishment from an entirely different crop. Maybe you're a field that needs to be fallowed—leaving the soil unsown with seeds of expectation for a growing season or more. When biodiversity leaves the soil, the nutrients leave with it, so little can grow unless it is heavily fertilized. This often produces an acceptable yield, but it doesn't restore the nutrients that make the soil what it is: a source of effortless, natural growth. Imitation rest leaves your body in the same position.

One of the most common misconceptions about rest for the producer is that rest is something to achieve, when in reality, rest is something you can only receive. There's a paradox here because you can't *will* yourself into relaxation, you can only soften into it and give yourself more and more permission for it. Think of it as being restored, not restoring yourself.

Rest is surrender. That word might sound alarming, but consider what you are being asked to surrender. You are surrendering being the one who has to hold tasks like belongings. Surrender is the acknowledgment that your will is not the only force in the world keeping life together.

In rest you might be highly attentive to the ten different kinds of birdcalls outside your window, or you might move your body around the house like a languid squid.

But whatever it is you are doing as you drop the demands to produce and optimize, if only for a moment, this much is true: if it's not restorative, it's just a pause, not rest.

59

To be honest, it's uncomfortable for the ego to be restored, because it wants to be the only one who can do anything worthwhile. To receive nourishment without strain is kind of an insult, or that's how the ego sees it. When you let go of your effort, you are agreeing that you are a human and not omnipotent and God-like.

The paradox is that in embracing your limits, you get more life back. This is the opposite of everything we are taught in production land, where limits are only liabilities, and the illusion of seamlessness is the cheap substitute for abundance.

You have to set your will down a little in order to rest, to embrace the composting part of your life where all of the unconscious materials and minerals get to form fertile soil. You get to leave decisions alone for a while.

It is letting everything mulch so that nutrients can be absorbed. That is why rest is not a nice-to-have for a maker: it is food. As a maker, you are always restoring the world. Without rest, we can only fix, not enliven.

What is restful for you—the way you soften into simply being—is subtle, specific, and changing. It will be qualitatively different from your lover's or your neighbor's way of resting.

Since the maker's rest responds to the body's inner knowing, it often looks less like spa vacations and more like connecting the self to the soft stuff of the world without agenda or transaction. Sometimes that looks like a very low-stakes expression: a loud sing-along in the car, a long conversation with your brother, an evening tending to simmering soups. At other times, it's relaxed observation: engrossing yourself in people-watching with open, nonjudgmental eyes or staring out the window at nothing in particular.

What shifts your gaze from the laser focus on what's new to the soft peripherals of all that is already here? Feel the nubby carpet or prickling pine needles under your feet.

WORK/NOT-WORK

Productivity land has only two categories for your time and effort: work and not-work.

Unproductive time becomes not-working time, a feeling of being in an airport waiting for your next flight, which in this case is your next performance of responsibilities. No one feels restored. No one has more energy. No one feels more like themselves after hanging out in an airport lounge no matter how many massage chairs they sit in or magazines they read.

Any work we do without a "ta-da" at the end, without a product, gets lumped into not-work. That's why the efforts of caregivers, who tend to living beings, are so easily overlooked and underpaid, and maternity leave can be mistakenly called a "vacation."

It's easy to think we're looking for more not-working time, which we probably are. Yet the richest among us can hire people to fold their laundry, cook their meals, clean up the kitchen, dress their small kids, and go to the grocery store so they can do all the recreational activities one can do on a boat—but as long as they still think of themselves as producers, they are not more restored, at a soul level, than anyone else.

Their days might be filled with leisure, but that doesn't give them more life. The flight from work has its own kind of discomfort.

The work/not-work binary is one reason it's so hard to "find time" for making, whether you are throwing together a collage, writing long letters to someone you appreciate, or lifting a sign at a protest. Making does not fit into either category.

Making takes effort, but not the kind we're used to as we put out fires and react to notifications. Making will cause you to scrunch your brow as you approach a new problem. You rouse yourself to sit in your chair with the intention to be with your own thoughts. It takes effort to dial your senator's office, to go for a walk with the intention of being with each step instead of trying to get somewhere. You might need to gather supplies, to close the door to your room on a weekend instead of going grocery shopping. Is it also effort to stare out the window and mull over what's next? Yes.

It's also beyond work, in that making does not demand a result in order to matter and does not respond well to force. It's beyond work in that a maker is often asked to let go of what they expect. A maker is free from the expectation that they will know in advance every possible step. Making is beyond work because it asks for presence over product. Bring the intention and release the expectation.

Walk to let your thoughts loose with the expectation that the clouds and the trees will give you new ones. Stare out the window. Chop vegetables. Close your email and dial the phone number, type the letter, or sketch. Weed the flower beds. Go to a coffee shop and drink tea and expect to find the person at the table next to you inspiring your short story. Turn the music up in your living room and move the sofa.

This is how we make time. At the end of the day, you will have reminded yourself of who you are: one who not only works but receives and gives in equal measure from the life of the world.

PROCRASTINATION

On the way to the car to take my daughter to preschool every morning, she bolts from me down the sidewalk. I don't run after her, knowing she will only go two houses down, then back. I suppose I could resist her, arguing every morning that she must go straight into her car seat, but that would add resistance on top of resistance. She is, in a very intelligent way, procrastinating. She does not do it consciously, but her body bubbles with anticipation at the transition to school. Running it off is a genius way of working with herself.

In the self-help world to which I belong, the word *procrastination* is usually accompanied by the phrase "how to overcome"; it's as if we've all agreed that procrastination is an enemy plotting to ruin all our plans. It obviously has to be cured and conquered. This is how we have been trained to "win"—by attacking anything in between us and what we should be doing.

As a producer, when you procrastinate, your inner middle manager berates the rest of you for what you're not doing. You're not simply resisting action; you are resisting your own resistance to action. Two equal and opposite forces within you have locked horns. No wonder you're exhausted.

To a stranger looking in from the outside, it might look like there's no difference between rest and procrastination. Both look like not-work, downtime. The difference is internal; what separates rest and procrastination is how we relate to our resistance.

Do whatever it is you do when you're procrastinating on purpose, and it turns into a choice. "We will schedule our procrastination this week," I told a group of makers. Whether it was puttering around the house or watching YouTube videos, they put an activity that they associated with resistance on the calendar. Reporting back the next week, one of the makers chose to scroll their phone, then noticed that they stopped sooner than usual—because they let themselves choose to start in the first place. It's almost as if choosing to start "procrastinating," instead of resisting the impulse and doing it anyway, reminds them of their power to make, or not make, however they like.

If procrastination is resistance to our resistance, then procrastinating on purpose helps us to see what our resistance is really about.

Procrastination knows something our doing self doesn't get yet. For my daughter running down the sidewalk, it's nervousness. All she needs is to move her body and take back a sense of autonomy in a situation where she's being herded into a car seat.

I love how insistent our procrastination is, the way it will not lie to us about what is going on inside. Maybe your procrastination is revenge upon an unrealistic pressure. The term "revenge bedtime procrastination," first popularized in China, described a pattern in which workers went to bed late after a long workday and a six-day workweek. The writer Daphne K. Lee described it as "a phenomenon in which people who don't have much control over their daytime life refuse to sleep early in order to regain some sense of freedom during late night hours."[1]

Should that need for freedom be overcome, or trusted? If we focused on ending the procrastination instead of investigating it, we would have lost the chance to fully meet that worthy need.

You might be procrastinating not only to take back power or to avoid discomfort but also to avoid the so-called pleasant emotions.

Maybe you're deeply excited about what your inner knowing is nudging you to do, but excitement sits uncomfortably next to your image of yourself as a responsible adult. That was the case for me when starting one of my first group programs. The idea filled me with so much energy at first, until one morning I hit a wall of procrastinating resistance. I heard myself complain to friends and in my journal pages, "I'm so not excited to do this." But when I find myself circling around the same stuck point, repeating the same complaint, that's usually a clue that my procrastination is really an upside-down desire. In that case, I was *very* excited, and that made me uncomfortable. My resistance was not to be "overcome" but cozied up with.

Instead of battling against my reluctance, I started to listen closely to its silent language. What was it that excited me so much about the group program that it scared me? Was it the fear of excitement itself, of stepping into a larger version of myself, of being seen and heard more loudly than ever before? As I continued to journal and reflect, the shell broke open on its own. I began to see that excitement and responsibility could coexist harmoniously. They were not opposing forces but complementary ones, each adding depth and color to the other.

In this light, procrastination is not just a delay in action (horror of horrors), but a pause for introspection, a moment to align our actions with our deepest desires and truths.

DOING MORE TO AVOID LIFE

Be very suspicious when your mind draws red circles around your many obligations. This urgency to produce gives you a sense of gravity, of self-importance, a belief that the world would fall apart without you.

If you have ever planned a day of rest only to spend it anxiously anticipating what tasks tomorrow will bring, you know how magnetic the obligations can be. I both love and hate the email notifications popping up on a Saturday while waiting in line at a busy coffee shop. There's something addictive about how a looming deadline makes me feel a superficial sense of order in the midst of the chaos of my life. Yet this may be a sign that you and I do not stay busy simply because we have to; we often stay busy to avoid the dizziness of the world; we stay busy to avoid looking at the chaos around us; we stay busy to keep a tight lid on life.

A popular Twitter account in the 2010s called @Horse_Ebooks posted absurdist tweets that went viral for being accidentally profound, but none was more popular than this post: "everything happens so much." It was retweeted thousands of times and even printed on T-shirts, capturing a #relatable mood. My friends and I sent it to each other when the other was beside themselves as a nod of sympathy.

Sharing the phrase was doing the work of noticing: rather than distracting ourselves from this "everything," now we were smiling at it, sitting with the chaotic state of the world and our relationship to it.

You can hear "everything happens so much" as a complaint—as in, there's so much to do; how can I keep up with it? But I'm curious about how it could bring us instead into a state of presence, of awareness of ourselves in the world in a given moment, the way we might whisper it as if we were sitting on a mountaintop with the perspective of distance, looking at the lively hustle and bustle of the town and the babbling brook. Everything happens so much. With us and without us.

Everything happens so much. Yet you exist. Baby sea turtles leave tracks on the sand as they make their way to sea for the first time. Future arms dealers and kindergarten teachers are being born in the same hour. A plane crashes into the ocean and a neighbor hangs dazzling Christmas lights. This sheer "muchness." The intricate layers in a rose, and vast tectonic shifts.

My mother-in-law told me that my husband, as a toddler, would cry in the backseat when his parents sang in harmony. It was just too intense, too beautiful, not to burst.

This "muchness" is just as intense and profound inside ourselves as it is out in the world.

When you fear your downtime, when you fear what you would do without the superficial order of deadlines, when you fear who you'd be if you weren't constantly doing things for others, you are in part avoiding the muchness, the mysteriousness, the unpredictability within you.

As producers, we are avoiding living.

You might avoid living because then you feel you'd have a dizzying number of choices to make.

You might avoid living because you carry a pulsing, unacknowledged pain and call it unacceptable—an unhappy lover, an ill-fitting job, or migraines.

You might avoid living because you believe the vast multiplicity that you feel within you is weird, other, unwelcome, unmarketable, unpopular, or uncool. Because your living might be inconvenient.

You might avoid living because you fear your own order. You fear the reality of your free ability to create sense from perceived chaos.

When you leave behind the superficial order of "doing," you are immediately confronted with the bracing reality of your own freedom to be, to approach the world with all the mysterious and messy truth of your heart.

DOING OUR DESIRES

If you had asked me what my desires were while I was working at a magazine in New York trying to "make it" in the city, I would've said nothing. Or, I want a cocktail. I want a promotion. I want to live in an apartment with one roommate instead of two plus a roommate's boyfriend who leaves his cereal bowls in the sink. That's why, when my mother asked me to take a trip with her because we had not spent time close together in years, I said maybe later. I was too busy trying to not fail, or trying to get a short-term win, to want anything that felt so extra, so luxurious.

In theory, of course a discounted flight to Iceland sounded lovely, but I could not let myself feel any desire for it because it had no short-term use for me. As horrifying as it is to admit, I couldn't even file it under a useful category in my mind called "making memories" or "getting enviable pictures for Instagram." I was trying to stay so productive that I could not see two inches past my nose.

After a few particularly gnarly weeks including a breakup, paperwork delays threatening my visa, and an argument between my friends, I hit a wall. I absolutely could not keep holding my breath until I accumulated enough "wins." A new direction slowly dawned on me: If I never get anywhere else other than where I am now, what would be worth it for me to respond to? What would I actually want to do? I booked the tickets that day.

Desire is a problem in the land of production. As a producer, your wants and needs must be kept far apart. They must live in different houses.

On one hand, producers are highly encouraged to indulge in the short-term gratification of buying stuff. Desires are allowed when it's time to consume: easy-to-grab lunches, highly specific ads targeted to you based on your search history. You can "want" quickly, so long as you come to work and maintain your regular hours. You can want compulsively—any addiction will do—so long as those wants don't make it harder for you to produce.

Producers can desire what it takes to stay productive, but anything beyond that is a luxury. This is a stressful place to be, because desire is energy and energy cannot be destroyed, according to thermodynamics, only transformed into another form of energy. So we do somersaults to justify desires, and advertisements will give us ways to justify and channel them. In fact, we *need* the newest noise-canceling headphones to keep producing.

A desire is also uncomfortable for your producer self because you can't hold the sensation in your body without *doing* something about it. If you feel a twinge of longing at an influencer's photos in Bali, you have a few options. You can either *earn and justify* a vacation by hustle and saving or *make the desire go away* by fulfilling it as quickly as possible. Pull out the credit card so the twinge turns into a hit of dopamine. Or, you can deny it wholesale, push it into the darkest corner of your mind. Who goes to Bali anyway? Not *my* kind of person.

But your desires are dangerous to the productive world when they draw you away from spending your life producing "value" for the current order.

So you are taught to rank your desires: Which ones are truly non-negotiable needs and which ones are extra nice-to-haves? Which ones can you squeeze in with the *real* obligations and which can be safely ignored? The special ones will be reserved for your two weeks of vacation or slipped between the virtuous billable hours. As a producer, your wants cannot be mysterious or open-ended. They cannot be inconvenient or "too much" compared to the others in your class and demographic. Otherwise, they are selfish, indulgent, childish, weird.

As a producer, you must take your desires *literally*, so as to deal with them as quickly as possible. If you feel a pang of wanting at the sight of children playing with their family in the front yard, you must want children. Now you have to make decisions about your family planning, or reject the feeling entirely. But your inner knowing may be leaping at the playfulness you saw, not the specific shape of that family.

Producers have been taught that meeting needs is competitive rather than collaborative. Since you don't *want* to have to compete, you relegate any perceived extras to the corner. For the maker, desires and needs are not different, they are forms of your humanity.

Maybe you really *do* want a trip to Bali, or maybe you want to put your feet in the earth, and the glossy photos online reminded you of that feeling. A maker gets to trust the essence of their desires without needing to fix them like a problem. Without the obligation to fix, a maker gets to get close enough to their desire to trust where it guides them.

"Why are you taking this route home and not the faster one?" asks the doing self. Because I want to, says the maker. "Why are you calling that friend you haven't spoken to in months? They don't even live around you anymore." Because I long to, the maker replies. "Why would you grow those flowers, gift your time, write that poem, restore the old car?" Because desire is leading me toward it, and I will see what comes.

CERTAINTY

Certainty is currency in the land of productivity. If you are what you do, you better be sure of what you choose to do. If you have any desire to stay away from failure and mitigate some risk, find something certain.

This is why, as a producer, you lead with your thinking mind above all else. Not only have you been taught to trade in certainties, you are taught to cling to what a cognitive mind cannot ever be truly certain of, like the future.

You also live in an information economy, which means that at every minute of the day, someone can profit when you believe that you don't know enough. The market *loves* when you look outside of your wisest, most curious self for an answer for what to do next, because that means it has your attention. The market can then sell you that bullet journal, app, or course to get you the very answers you've been looking for. So much the better if you don't even have to look, when the software can anticipate your question before you ask it.

This kind of knowing is part and parcel of a larger problem in the land of productivity—our lives are seen as objects separate from soul. Our selves and our relationships become manipulatable products—external things, easier to shape according to predefined standards. This dynamic is easiest to spot on the playground of social media, where we curate our lives into pixelated avatars. Each post, photo, or status update looks like a fragment of a flat identity, filtered and polished for public consumption, then fed back to us through ads. But tech companies did not invent the way we make ourselves into products that are either working or not working, five stars or one.

Attempting to give our humanity the fixity of a product or a data point is what Max Weber called rationalization, what Georg Lukaçs meant by reification, what Hannah Arendt called alienation from the world. In the realm of "producing knowledge," this alienation extends to an obsession with objectivity and neutrality.

My students in undergraduate writing came ready to find bias in news sources. This lens of critique is among the first they reach for. The point was to point out how our muddy personal perspective would get in the way of *real* knowledge. Their job, as they saw it, was to spot how a source's humanity was getting in the way of actual facts.

In the best class I ever took, a distinguished poet handed us scruffy students a heavy spiral-bound packet of poems. In it the likes of Emily Dickinson and Dante wondered about the nature of time, God, suffering, and the existence, or not, of the afterlife. Not only was the poetry intimidating (isn't it what we were all forced to pretend to understand in high school?), the subject matter wasn't exactly casual cocktail party subject matter. Nor was it anything we could be certain about. But the poet did something remarkable: he asked us if the words seemed true to our experience. Even bolder, he actually wanted to know our response, as if it would make a difference for his life too.

Our job was a simple one, though not always easy: we read the poems and wrestled with them like Jacob grappled with an angel in the book of Genesis. We were not to pick them apart, but *contend* with them. Not prove them right or wrong, or explain them. But to notice what was alive and dead in us and on the page. That was our task: aliveness.

What if we looked at our time that way: Is it alive? If not, why not? If the answer is no, that doesn't mean we must make it alive again. We must see why. Maybe it was alive, but something has changed.

Productivity describes the way we turn our time and effort into things, but the maker has a relational view of life. His certainty is a decision about who he already is in connection to the gifts and needs of the world. Certainty about his next step emerges from a maker as an artifact of this relationship. Certainty looks less like a mental calculation and more like the trust that forms after you have traveled miles with someone.

In the productive mode, you have to be sure of yourself, your methods, or the results. Ideally all three. You have to be sure that you will not let it fail, or your tools will not fail, that the odds will remain in your favor, that the result will be yours. As a maker, you are learning not to use this form of useful intelligence against your own humanity.

In quantum mechanics, the uncertainty principle states that you can't be sure of both a particle's position and momentum; you have to choose between knowing one or the other. The surer you are about how fast it's going, the less sure you are about where it is, and vice versa.

Production land denies this principle by trying to control the desired result and the way to get there at the same time. That faux-certainty simply doesn't work when you're dealing with any new or living being. A producer can be sure about what tactics they will choose, like a pickup artist using the same line on a dozen women at the bar, but they can't guarantee the response.

A maker can observe from both directions without trying to control either. They can stake a claim on where they want to go, a vision driven by desire, and explore different ways to get there.

Or a maker can embrace their desired way of working, the road they want to travel: like street photography, connecting their friends, or taking the trail on the left, then surrender to where it takes them.

A maker is not certain that they are objectively the best ones for a job, only that they are who they are, and they see what they see, and they love what they love.

A maker does not need infallible tools to achieve the result, though they treat their tools with respect because they work with what is, with what they have, and they trust that they will have what they need when they need it.

The maker's trust comes not from rigid plans or infallible methods but from staying awake. She is like a sailor reading the stars and the sea, knowing she cannot control the ocean's currents.

INSTRUCTIONS

Producers often struggle with big decisions, and too many decisions feel big.

The middle manager in your mind can tell you what to do, but rarely have you been listened to long enough for you to discern where your inner knowing is leading you now, which may be different than a year ago.

You've been given responsibility for a lot of decisions but not the discernment to choose between them. You have been offered really good advice, but it never seems to get you to that fully creative life that you sense is possible.

You've come up with many ideas for what you might want, but your parents' way of getting there, or your competitor's way, or your best friend's way, doesn't work for you.

When my baby first arrived earthside, screaming like a howler monkey, I was transported to a new planet with unfamiliar customs, rhythms, and languages. On planet parenthood, it was my job to tend to the world's most vulnerable creature who I loved so much it physically hurt. I just wanted to know what to do to get parenting right.

While pregnant, I lumbered into classes on breastfeeding and respectful parenting. I did chest compressions on a doll in case my actual baby ever choked.

I furrowed my brow while reading online forums full of advice, terrifying anecdotes, conflicting philosophies on everything from what to eat (both me and the baby) and how to sleep (both me and the baby). Everyone had advice, and none of it could tell me how to be.

Having a child is a wild, creative act that we've collectively tried to tame into a doomed self-improvement project—with just the right theories, just the right tools, the right methods, we've made parenthood into an end that can be *achieved*. Our life is an equally wild, creative act we've tried to tame into a doomed self-improvement project.

It's not doomed because we cannot evolve but because we cannot evolve with mere doing. Creating happens when we've unlearned how everything is supposed to go. Creating requires responding to what is: improvising with reality. Of course, we need skills to improvise with. A pianist learns the scales until they are unconscious muscle memories. But employing skills is not the same thing as making with them.

The maker learns to put the instructions in their rightful place: how to tie a shoe, how to read, how to build a bridge that won't collapse or prevent infection while performing surgery.

A producer continues to treat themselves as a student in a never-ending high school who just needs to pass the next test before they graduate.

"Tell me what to *do*." It's an understandable desire because our energy is naturally flowing; you are not meant to spin in place or to be an object gathering dust.

You can give someone a structure for the sake of structure, but a structure doesn't create a result, a spirit, a feeling.

Consider dating advice. The best dating advice—the most succinct, no-fail advice for dating is "be yourself." That's always going to be true because if you *didn't* date as yourself, any relationship that did grow would be inauthentic and counterproductive to love. But such advice is not, in the words of production land, "actionable." Being yourself is not something to *do*, it's a way of being. Your self is not a series of habits, styles, and techniques that have gotten you where you are.

You can live someone else's life if you do what they tell you. You can build someone else's business under your own name, have someone else's ideal family, write someone else's preferred book. And it will feel terrible. If you get the result you wanted from the "right steps," if they're not authentic to you, you will feel like a fraud. If you don't get the result you expected, you will feel ashamed. This is a step-by-step process to hating everything.

Good advice will feel like freedom. It will always, in its way, show a maker how it's possible to be; it will open a door they didn't see or thought was locked.

A maker sees advice like a painter sees color on the palette, as material to play with, not as a prescription to cure an illness. You do not need to be cured.

EFFICIENCY

In 1944, the Office of Strategic Services (the predecessor of the CIA) produced the *Simple Sabotage Field Manual*, a document for destroying rebellious organizations. The document explained how undercover saboteurs could reduce an organization's efficiency so it would collapse under the weight of its own labor. The list of recommendations is full of conspicuous *doing*, suggesting they refer "back to matters decided upon at the last meeting and attempt to reopen the question of the advisability of that decision" and "think out ways to increase the number of movements necessary on your job: use a light hammer instead of a heavy one."[1]

The logic of efficiency would seem to solve for the least amount of effort for the greatest amount of reward. But when applied to questions of our personal growth, efficiency does the opposite. It starts to look more like the above CIA program, weighing us down under a mountain of actions that look like movement but take us nowhere.

A successful photographer I worked with was advised by those "in the know" that she should really be a business coach, teaching other photographers to make money themselves. So she did. She signed clients and served them well, but the role fit her like an itchy sweater. She was a healer and an artist at heart, so she snuck those passions in the side door of her business by soothing her clients' anxieties and creating beautiful images for her marketing. After all, making money and telling others how to make money was, on the surface, the most efficient route to growing her business.

But the efficient route to another person's life is very slow indeed. The photographer had to hype herself up every day just to keep her business running, even though it was "working" according to her balance sheet. When she needed to make decisions like how and where to advertise, she agonized over the details, taking course after course from experts. All the "smart" answers had to come from outside.

Seeing how inefficient her efficient strategy had become, she was willing to steer the ship in a new direction no matter how slowly it turned. Little by little, she adjusted her offerings to fit with who she really was. Instead of luring in clients with a promise of a return on financial investment, she offered them what she loved to create. Her relationship with her business shifted from a complicated math problem to a collaborative art project. She felt warmer toward her clients, since they could now fall in love with her and her vision, not simply what result she could get for them. And it did not take long for her to see that the responses from her clients were so much more powerful than when she was "efficient."

As my client discovered, aiming for the fastest route is a deeply inefficient way to live. All the errant *doing* masquerades as efficiency; it passes for, but isn't, growth. It distracts you from what you're actually trying to grow: yourself, what you love, your business, your art practice, and so on. When efficiency rules the day, you misdirect yourself from what actually matters to you.

The maker's path that I propose is not about going faster or slower but aiming straight into the heart of the truth. That directness is its own kind of efficiency.

The truth might be that nothing is clear at all; you don't know what to do next, and all choices look equally plausible. Then the perfectly efficient thing to do is to actively raise the antennae so you might hear the source within you—your inner knowing—when it speaks.

On the surface, nothing appears to be happening. But you know you are making yourself ready to leap at the perfect time.

DOING "BALANCE"

After your workday, your care tasks, filling your stomach, letting the dog out, changing your shirt because you spilled coffee on it, replying to texts and emails until your day is simply *over*, with no delightful discovery or shared belly laugh or deep sigh of contentment to be found, you are told you need balance. Don't overwork yourself (lest you burn out and need to quit), but don't be apathetic.

The problem with the need for balance is how it becomes a task of situating yourself in the middle ground between two problematic extremes. Not too happy or too sad, not too intense but not lazy. This balance keeps both "problems" exactly as they are, perfectly intact, at arm's length. Once again, to the producer, balance is yet another virtue to *achieve*.

Balance in production land means doing the right amount of everything. Just enough time at work, but not so much to become "problematic," enough hobbies to be interesting without being weird. This kind of balance simply suggests evenness, avoiding extremes.

Yet a photograph without high tones and shadows does not hold our attention for very long. It looks dull. In the same way, production land turns an ambient fluorescent light on the whole day.

On a physiological level, balance is not evenness; evenness is a sign of death. A body with *even* hormones is a dead body. True balance is a dynamic state that works with contrast, not a static hold. In yoga, you'll hear the phrase "root to rise." Feel the gravity of your heels on the ground before reaching up.

Production land does not support this contrast because it demands that we keep up. A producer is coiled so tightly to hold on, she doesn't experience a wide range of herself, let alone tolerate contrasts that seem inefficient.

You can't feel fully, creatively human unless you can tolerate deep shadow and light at once, because our days on a most basic level require both. A time to start, a time to end. A time to run full out, a time to melt into bed. A time to scream, a time to laugh.

I remember when my sister called me from a hospital bed to say it was cancer, how the minutes after repeating "I love you" pulled long and thin like taffy. I watched a light fixture mesmerize a squirming baby in her mother's arms as the sirens blared outside the windows. The train conductor announced each stop with such boredom while I could feel the blood pulse through my feet. How horrible, ordinary, and shining everything was.

That's true every minute.

If managing balance is not the goal, we are free to ride the contrasts that make up our days and who we are. Because contrast does not only define our time; it defines us.

As we grow older, we tend to get wise to our extremes. Maybe we see our quick temper so we modulate our tone, or we think we're too loud so we turn the volume knob to five and keep it there. We know that we have a tendency to be quiet in meetings, so we make a note to speak up at least once or twice. This so-called balance is just scrambling to compensate for apparent weakness. You do not become more flexible or human or dynamic in your range, just better managed.

Inevitably, I come to adore every one of the makers I work with for their paradoxical traits: bold and tender, quiet and mischievous, ambitious and sensitive. Isn't that what happens when we love anyone? We see they hold an impossible combination of apparent paradoxes that we have never quite found before.

A maker is not required to smooth out his quirks into a featureless expanse. He may be all of it—the responsible one and the adventurer, the analyzer and the social butterfly, the sinner and the saint.

His balanced life doesn't mimic the clock's dull tick but echoes the ocean's tides—sometimes calm, sometimes stormy, but always pulsing with life.

FORCE

"If I don't ___, then I'll never ____." "I have to ___, or else ____."

The motivation for productivity runs on the threat of shame to encourage action. When it does not work, you feel the threat and run from it. When it does work, you get to use shame or fear anytime you want to be motivated.

You are a maker, not a soldier heading into battle. You are not a Chevy with its rear wheels five inches deep in mud that just needs a little shove. Your nervous system does not like to be pushed off a cliff while being told how brave you are for jumping.

You are always, in part, a nervous child. You would not scream "You screwed up! You froze!" at a seven-year-old on the soccer field. Whether she gritted her teeth or ran away the next time, she would hear that refrain each time she went to kick the ball.

Do not force your nervous system with your mind. Don't shove yourself out of planes or waterboard yourself with "you should" and "you ought" and "or else"—even for the loveliest cause. Because inner violence can't make more life.

As a maker, you must play first with what *is* rather than what *should* be, including your own nervous and worst thoughts. You do not shove your ugliest doubt—"I should have become a dentist; everyone will unfriend me and write reviews telling me they've known I'm a fraud"—into a box. You do not even fire your inner critic for being the worst-producing employee.

Even the meanest one—the one who reminds you of what you did in middle school and blames you every time you get a cold. Even *that* inner critic doesn't get abused. You do not assault yourself with fake smiles when you're really shaking, or tighten your fists around the doubt. You do not add cruelty to your fear.

If you force yourself, your inner knowing will rebel. Your body will send you messages with everything it can. You will get migraines. You will develop carpal tunnel. Your surroundings will conspire to distract you from all your doing. You will get ants in your kitchen, or your water heater will go kaput.

Force is a symptom of distrust. The cure to forcing yourself is not giving up or abandoning your intentions because they got too hard, but closeness. Spend time getting to know the desires behind your resistance without making them wrong. Sidle up to why you wanted to try in the first place. Touch your real intentions, the ones that were forgotten amid all your plans.

DOING THE BEST

For a producer, ambition is about winning and losing. If you set a lofty vision for achievement, you can only either get there or fail. This all-or-nothing prospect is lethal for the maker.

How many things have you not done because you couldn't imagine reaching a high score? Nothing can ever really be the best unless it pushes past the edge of what has been done before, putting the producer in the position of constantly competing against themselves as well as others.

At some point when I was a kid, I only wanted to do things if I could win at them. I loved dancing, but a teacher told me I was bowlegged, so that was off the table. I wanted to be a writer, so I had to be the next Shakespeare or nothing at all. The desire to win was the only way I knew how to desire anything, so the "best" became the rubric for everything I did.

This was hard to sustain. And so, the land of productivity offered another option: not caring, settling for okay. *Okayness* is the comfort of not having to achieve anything at all, at least for a while. Numbing the pain after a loss.

In other words, the productive "best life" creates two opposing options: the one says aim for the version of you that transcends all your current limitations. It says, tune in to your best self. What does she speak like? What is his morning routine? Who do they hang out with? Do that.

When this fails, the other option kicks into gear. Forget achievement, success, too much aliveness in general. Embrace okayness—fair to middling. Use it as a kind of blanket. Not a *deep* okayness, the kind that arises from a profound acceptance of all that is, flaws and all. An okayness that is merely Not Too Much.

This okayness believes that the scope of your imagination is off. Bigger, better, faster does not work for you, so it must be that what you really want is *only smallness*. To learn to enjoy doing the dishes, to manage your corner of the office, to run your small institution like a fiefdom.

Under the doing model, the options are to overperform or console yourself with less. To do the best, or to do just enough.

At your "best," you are a temporary amplification of all your winning qualities and not a representation of your greatest wholeness. At your best, you're spinning ten plates on a unicycle; no one is disappointed in you and everyone oohs and aahs.

When those plates ultimately fall, your ambition falls with them. You go home, feed your cats, brush your teeth, and call it enough.

This double bind of "doing the best" and "doing enough" isn't rich enough to sustain us for very long.

The idea of "the best" turns our idealism into an object, an externally derived standard, instead of an internal North Star. The problem isn't ambition itself—I'd argue that our producer dreams are too small. No self-driving car or crowd of adoring fans will light up the soul.

Like the stars, the highest direction of inner knowing can both humble and thrill you. Outside a mere result, what way of being makes your heart swell at the thought of it?

Maybe your deepest ambition is to create beauty in the face of chaos. Maybe it's to feel connected to every human you speak to. Maybe it's to make harmony where there's been only suspicion.

Maybe it's to love every seemingly unlovable part of the world, including the parts of you that aren't very loving.

If your life could be characterized by one quality above all, what would it be? This possibility should have you quaking in your boots and warm your heart at once.

Even if you never got there for a minute, your life would be cast in the light of that shining possibility.

DOING THE PLAN

In high school, I craved a leading role in the musical *My Fair Lady*. The auditions were held in the darkened auditorium. We watched each other climb one by one from the audience seats to the bright stage and sing, "I could have danced all night." We whispered and watched carefully, calculating our chances of getting the only role worth having, Eliza Doolittle. I found the tension so unbearable that I quipped, "Wouldn't it be funny if someone tripped?"

Then it was my turn. I cleared my throat, scooted past my fellow wannabe Elizas. As I climbed the stairs, my sneaker caught on the stage's lip, throwing me headlong under the spotlight. Silence from the auditorium. I decisively brushed off the knees on the black jeans I wore to be sophisticated before stepping to the microphone and staring into the darkness of the auditorium. I swallowed and belted in my best fake British accent, "I could have daahhhnced all naaaaaht." Hands shaking, I climbed back down into the rows of seats where my classmate whispered, "Did you fall on purpose?" "Yes," I assured her. I did not get the role.

Most of us are not doing anything on purpose. Most of us are too tired from decisions about what to consume or about our master plan. Most of our actions are cocktails of guesswork, habit, and social expectation. We do not admit this.

Why is it, then, that other people always seem to walk in a straight line, with their eyes focused on an invisible point on the horizon, like they don't need a map and never did? They walk with an imaginary purpose because wandering is not a socially acceptable hobby like golf. Golf is very expensive walking and aiming. Rarely do we allow ourselves to noodle around without a return on investment, let alone admit it.

Other people always sound like they know the answer, but those are just the sounds we make to each other when we're sitting around the table. We don't bring up the years we gave to a boss we hated, or the emails we never sent, or the nights spent trying to impress our friends we don't like that much. We hide the time labeled "wasted" from each other, and in doing so, we accidentally lie.

The impact of this is that it looks like everyone else is the main character in an epic tale written by a subtle genius, whereas we're the sidekick in a low-budget sitcom written by a drunk and quarreling room of writers who have fully run out of ideas.

I've seen many people, myself included, refuse to heed the call of their inner knowing because they can't find a good plan. "I don't know what will happen after I'm finished, so I will not start."

This is not to say that there's no place for a plan. We want our contractors and surgeons to have a solid one. But their importance has been greatly exaggerated in the land of productivity. The pressure to pretend that you have answers distracts you from finding real guidance. This guidance will not come from your doing but from moments when your doing breaks down.

Why is it that we grow most profoundly when all our best-laid plans fall apart? When our most carefully designed schemes are undone?

Sometimes we find ourselves there by accident, when our body fails, our car runs off the road, we fall in love, or we get fired. This is a key part of every cycle of organic life: it is necessary decay. If nothing decayed, broke down, was digested, we could not absorb the nutrients of our food.

And the good news is that this process doesn't have to be unconscious or accidental. The best path to growth, paradoxically, is often found in a conscious harnessing of exactly this kind of state. Let's call it "undoing."

PART II

UNDOING

If I Am Not What I Do,
How Will I Know
What to Do?

AN INTRODUCTION TO HUMAN BEING

You still might want me to tell you what to do now to stop merely producing and act like a maker. I would, if I were you. Even the most rebellious by nature crave a clear list of steps, even if only to name, very specifically, what they will *not be doing*.

If a miracle occurred, you might try my hypothetical steps. For that reason, I really must not tell you what to do, because then you might be distracted from what is already growing in you.

In the quest to become a maker beyond all your producing, you are dealing with a deep pattern, so it's not enough to change your thoughts about your efforts. You can't just make a New Year's resolution to take a pottery class or a promise to "actually rest more" this time; there is no foolproof plan approved by experts.

Until you trust who you really are underneath your producer's clothes, your imagination will be hijacked by the dominant cultural narrative, and you will find a way to get back to your productive self regardless of what else you do.

So don't just try to do less. Don't just try to do better. Don't spend your time embroidering clothes that don't fit.

No matter how long you've been upholding the laws of the land of production, that does not touch who you are. Sit back; I only want to convince you that your very being is a creative miracle apart from your doing. As you read this, your fingernails are growing. Your body weight leaves an imprint on the chair. Someone sees you out of the corner of their eye and has a thought they've never thought before.

Your being is who you are before you do anything at all.

Before your words, your thoughts, your style, your brilliant ideas, your titles, your pain, your joy, the worst thing that ever happened, the best day of your life, before, during, and after, you simply *are*.

This is the seat of your humanity. Ask yourself: Who are you *being* when you are doing nothing? Who are you being before you've done anything and after you're done? Ask your best friends. Your pets. They feel your presence and find it beloved.

That is why there is no such thing as doing *nothing*—the great sin of our culture—because there is no such thing as being nothing.

I want to convince you that the quality of being trumps your actions every time. Here waits your clearest awareness, the well from which you draw truth.

Even though the world is not going to applaud a human for trusting her being (except for those whose capacity for being allows them to see it), therein lies your power to make a life. The world is not going to give out awards for the results of this trust.

And by the time you get to the results, and you do create all the tiny masterpieces with your days, by the time the applause reaches your ears, it won't matter because you—really, you—were there the whole time.

INNER KNOWING

Without the guidance of production land to tell us what to do, what are we left with?

We're squeezed from the serene warmth of the womb into a world brimming with demands. We absorb a clear message: follow these lines, stay in character, and you might just find your way back to a sense of safety and belonging. So we adopt personalities, select our opinions in the hopes that they will save us from our sense of separateness. We learn to earn our keep, to prove our point of view, to sing for our supper. We know where to look for our cues.

But inside our fleshy, mortal bodies lives a compass whose needle always points to authentic aliveness: our indestructible inner knowing. This source of guidance was never much interested in applause.

"Inner knowing" might sound like an invention of the postmodern obsession with our individual *selves* and our *doing our own research*, but it's a bigger idea with deep roots. The ancient Greeks, for instance, called it *nous*, a quality of mind that grasps the order of life beyond our senses. Whether you call it human intuition, the Holy Spirit, or the *daimon* (another ancient Greek image), it's our guidance that goes beyond the superficial layers of information.

It's why a musician, after hearing a few notes, can play more than a melody but the song's emotional undercurrents and the story it tells.

For a scientist, it's the source of intuitive leaps that break open old ideas, when an "aha" emerges not just through experimentation and logic but through a hidden understanding of how things just "are."

Unlike the land of production, which can only be driven by data and scientific materialism, the inner knowing offers a more holistic, interconnected, and profound understanding of our world and ourselves.

In our frantic efforts to earn our place, we had to tune out this voice.

I was probably seven when I started to bury my inner knowing deep underground. After reading a little story I'd written, one grown-up worried they resembled a character a little too closely, so I toned down my tales, handwritten on ruled school paper, into words no one could worry about.

And I could tell it wasn't safe to "know" when something was amiss in the adult world, let alone share it. I would try to ignore things like the muffled, arguing voices I heard upstairs from my grandmother's basement since the grown-ups would just say, "Let's get ice cream!"

In a world fixated on the measurable, the material, and the computable, the practice of listening to our own knowing sounds like inefficient self-indulgence. Yet the alternative is to obey borrowed guidance, the same guidance that created the patterns and problems we want solutions to.

Mystics across traditions often spoke of this inner knowing as the divine spark within, an eternal flame that flickers in the depths of our being. It has a precision from left field that doesn't care if you can prove it.

I compared our inner knowing to a compass, because we experience its guidance from wherever we stand, but our inner knowing is not an individual *thing*. It's a collective pulse—a common stream that runs through all of us. It's not private property, but it speaks to us all in our own language, with our specific gifts and sensitivities.

This inner knowing calls us to connect our inner and outer lives, to live in harmony with the tune of our souls.

You see it in the hunch that nudges you to go left instead of right, the gut feeling that something you heard isn't quite the truth, or the rising swell of joy when you stumble upon a forgotten passion.

To attend to our inner knowing asks that we hold a lot of paradox. To follow it, we play with states that we've been taught we are to keep separate: vulnerability and strength, humility and audacity.

Fortunately and unfortunately, it doesn't shout with piercing beeps and notifications. Inner knowing has us listening to reality. It won't predict who will win the Super Bowl or tell you if your crush is "the one." Your inner knowing will not hand you a neatly packaged job title. It won't shield you from mistakes or let you avoid all heartbreak. In fact, it might lead you straight into the knotted parts of your life.

So why bother with your inner knowing?

Simply because it's the antitoxin to the poison offered by the land of production. What it does, and does better than any lie detector, is tell the truth of who you are. It will not solve all your problems, but it will show you the real ones to work with.

GREETING THE DOING SELF

The world will shout. That's just what it does as the land of productivity blasts Radio Do More. You take in hundreds of daily advertisements, not to mention cute emails "just circling back" and news alerts on the most recent heat wave, election speculation, celebrity breakup.

Try shutting your eyes and you'll find it's even noisier within the mind. In the brief moments between tasks, you can hear it arguing with itself over the agenda for what's next, what's best, what's missing.

We had to tune out our inner knowing to be good producers. But another part of our humanity is very attached to the programming of production land. It will never willingly shut it off.

I call it the "doing self," though it isn't one *thing*. It is a protective impulse within you that grasps for a manageable identity. You could call it the ego, cultural conditioning, the "personality," "nafs" in Sufism, our "base nature." I'm not a stickler for terminology.

I call it the doing self because it mistakes our identity for our outer actions. It loves Radio Do More, since it responds to urgent calls about anything it thinks will keep it alive: rising in fame, new levels of status, accumulating stuff, attaining moral perfection.

My doing self is the one who estimates the circumference of my pale arms and compares it to a stranger's toned biceps at the pool. It says I am the one who did not hit the gym enough. My doing self shouts "neener-neener" to high school nemeses. It says I am the one who left my hometown, so there.

Some days my doing self wants a luxurious flight to Paris, the kind where you sleep in a private pod and they bring you champagne as you survey the clouds. It wants to be the one who can buy a first-class ticket.

It hates waiting for others, yet it often arrives late because it hates to be inconvenienced. The doing self chooses goals based on the next obvious way to get recognition. The doing self loves a trophy case.

If I feel angry, it says I am an angry person, both wronged and righteous, on my way to heaven.

When I give money without explicitly asking for anything in return, it feels certain my candidacy for sainthood is inevitable. The doing self is swiftly flattered and even more quickly offended.

My doing self is sure about who I must be. It changes its story about who I must be by the second.

It's not very imaginative, since it only knows what's happened before. The past is the doing self's well-thumbed reference book. It answers any question by pulling out the dusty tome of How It's Been. The poor thing is always confusing what's happening for who you are, your experience for your essence.

If you want to stare your doing self squarely in the face, tell it that the world is waiting with open arms for your gifts. To believe your deepest visions belong here feels profoundly threatening to the doing self.

For the doing self, your inner knowing is very embarrassing. It makes you vulnerable to nature, other people, and bodily sensations. This creativity is disgustingly hopeful and uncynical. It's inefficient and unreasonable.

101

To the doing self, your inner knowing is recklessly curious about all your experiences, and a little ridiculous in its embrace of life as beautiful material. All of this, to the doing self, is a distraction from clutching an end result.

The doing self can come along as you create a richer life than it can imagine; you won't leave it behind. It helps us survive our world, keeping us functional. It knows how to take what is socially given and offer it up as usable material to other parts of the self. It is a miller of grist that other parts of the self need for growing, a wheel catching the current and making it available as energy. Your inner knowing can see this pretty clearly. Unfazed, it can listen to the doing self's complaints. Your inner knowing will show your doing self that the way to aliveness needs a different guide.

YOUR INNER KNOWING TELLS THE TRUTH

When you sense something is off, your doing self searches for a reason. You notice you're slower to laugh, more irritated at the traffic than you would normally be, but there are so many potential reasons and solutions, and *also*, barring a crisis, none of the problems are capital-s Serious enough to explain the nagging sense of what's wrong. But there must be something to fix.

Is it a lack of organization in your schedule? Too many emails? Maybe your friends live too far away and your colleagues are sticks in the mud. If your partner was in a better mood on the weekend, maybe you would be too. Just be more grateful. Put a gratitude journal in your shopping cart.

Any and all of those circumstances could be real, on one level, but the doing self can't see deeply enough to find the gold nugget of truth begging for your attention. Your inner knowing, on the other hand, already holds the truth of who you are and what is needed now.

A creative life thrives and withers in direct correlation with the truth. Not a mathematical truth or anything so provable—the truth of what is alive in you and what is not.

While the producer loves the next logical step, your inner knowing sees what is true *now*. It's not threatened by how convenient and comfortable the status quo might be—your inner knowing has no "winning" agenda, it simply *is*.

The truth does not drop breadcrumbs to fame and fortune but instead always leads to what is *fitting* for us. Fittingness is a genuine match to who we are now, not a borrowed cultural ideal we must squeeze into like the outfit on a store mannequin. This will always be more beautiful and particular than any success we could have bought off the rack.

The truth has a ring to it, even when it's painful. Think of when the heartbreak of leaving a relationship that's long over is easier to take than the pain of staying. The truth your inner knowing sees will tell you when to prune and when to shoot new leaves. It speaks with calm compassion:

"That hurt a part of you."

"That was unkind. You actually want to be kinder than that."

"This color is off."

"You are ready to move."

But beware how quickly your mind makes productive plans for what your inner knowing is telling you. As a child, I had a strong sense of justice, so my doing self latched on to the shiniest version of that truth: I should be a human-rights lawyer! (I should not.)

As an adult working at a magazine, an overwhelming gut feeling came over me at the office. The *sense* of the truth was: "You aren't supposed to stay here. Your vocation is spiritual." The only thing my doing self could conclude was, "I guess I should go be a priest." (I should not.) I wanted to turn the knowing into a task as quickly as possible.

But your inner knowing doesn't explain, doesn't whine, and doesn't argue. How annoying that your inner knowing does not justify itself in advance, but that is not its role. The doing self wants a justification, but none will come. Your inner knowing simply *is*. It will not demand your obedience, but it will not lie.

UNDOING OLD QUESTIONS

If we pause from asking "What do I do?" when we encounter another one of life's pathless forests, what do we ask instead? A more interesting question: *How am I being?*

The reason you want to do all the productive things is because you think that's the cost of your ticket to being who you already are. When you ask yourself what you want to experience after finally producing enough, you find that you are seeking the qualities that your inner knowing already has in spades: peace, connection, curiosity, wonder, generosity, to offer a short list.

If you want to know what your inner knowing is like, just ask what it is you hope to experience at the end of the day. Since our knowing is not a thing but a state, we feel it with our body. The lie of doing distracts us with the thought that we need to earn access to this state. But it is unearnable.

As doers, it is our daily tragedy to clean the bathroom only to see toothpaste on the mirror within the hour. Only from the presence of our inner knowing can we laugh and say "Oh well" to the doing self who so badly wants it done. Your inner knowing does not need a completed result.

Your inner knowing sees the bigger picture, the *quality* that you are doing all this stuff for. It is qualitative, not quantitative.

Inner knowing asks "What kind of day was it?" without labeling it a success or failure. All creative power draws from this presence. It is the seat from which we relate to reality.

When I was twenty-seven, my friends and I were all getting our hearts broken around the same time. Relationships we were sure were going to be our ticket to some standard of grown-up accomplishment were crumbling at our feet and we were left without that future in the form of a person.

We were all in graduate school, researching abstract topics like medieval cosmology through the lens of our loosely veiled personal pain. What would Thomas Aquinas think about the fact that this woman won't date me? I wonder if virtue ethics might have a little something to say about the guy in Alabama's inability to call me back.

I don't say this to mock us. We were earnestly trying so hard to figure out the right thing to do all the time, even as we could see it wasn't "working" in the real world. We could tell by how frustrated we were, trying to form the right plans, look the right way, and take the right steps.

But there are these beautiful crumbling moments when all our doing falls to pieces. The hidden gift: we don't have the energy to pick them back up again.

One of these moments found us gathering around the table at Archie's bar over beer and fries as we licked our wounds at the end of our semester. I stood up and offered a toast: "Here's to more interesting problems!" We laughed and clinked our pint glasses. We all understood what this meant. There's a whole world behind door number two, where we're no longer trying to get her back or answer a trick question. Let us welcome a chapter where our challenges are not an attempt to fix the same old pain. If we cannot avoid being unfinished, we may as well be unfinished in a new, more creative way.

We have our favorite unanswerable questions. We have usually asked them in every new room we've entered. Questions like,

"How can I make sure I don't fail?" "How can I make sure no one thinks I'm needy?" "How can I be the favorite?" They're like a tangled gold necklace we roll between our fingers hoping that will free the knot.

In Greek mythology, the Sphinx terrorized the people of Thebes with a riddle—"What being has four legs in the morning, then two legs at noon, and then three in the evening?"—destroying anyone who could not answer. Oedipus solved the riddle by answering, "Man, who crawls on all fours as a baby, then walks on two legs, and finally needs a cane in old age." For this, he became king.

Ancient myth is full of terrifying creatures who pose seemingly impossible questions to the characters on a journey. These questions represent a test—but not of brute strength or memorized facts. The heroes and heroines are called to use their deep imagination, their upside-down logic. Only when they see through the eyes of their imagination can they become who they are supposed to be. More interesting questions always call forth new ways of being, not simply new actions.

From your inner knowing, answer the riddle of production land: What happens when you're done? And then what? What way of being are you holding hostage under the ransom of more doing?

Once you ask what it is you think all this doing can get for you, you can see what your inner knowing is calling you to be. Whereas producers can't afford to be curious, or connected, or have fun since that might introduce inefficiencies, makers can *be* the hoped-for result *as they go*—in the process, the whole way.

UNDOING VICES

If you're anything like me or most of the makers I know, you are consuming to stuff down all that wants to be made through you. But what you consume and the way you feel when you consume it are not accidental. Your vices are hidden parts of your creative power that have been tamed.

You know that you are distracting yourself from your own brilliance. You can tell because of the subtle resentment that comes up when you entertain yourself by listening to the stories of others who have "gotten somewhere," while you catch a glimpse of yourself in the reflection of your phone.

But you feel helpless to do otherwise. Your distractions are keeping you afloat. You could be shamed by an app into seeing how much money you would save without your three glasses of wine habit, but that only works temporarily because your so-called vices are expressions of your inner knowing coming out sideways.

If you took away the eight-dollar iced latte and the second whiskey, your tendency to say "yes" to your brother's request when you mean no just to keep your weekends full, or the video game that went on for too long, you wouldn't be left with a better person. You would be without a way of showing up that your unconscious maker self needs.

Maybe you have a wild desire for visual experimentation that only expresses itself through online shopping. Maybe the way that you reached for your glass of wine was about a generative holy call to stop rushing and start feeling like music the way you did before you placed all the expectations on yourself.

Pay attention to how the distractions make you feel. Specifically, how you get to feel when you're doing that thing that you're not supposed to do and how that lets you be.

You want to slow down, but you don't know how without over-committing and then blaming other people for why you're tired. You want to share your unique experience of the world, and the safest way to do that is through commenting on other people's posts.

You want to cherish yourself, to be tender, so a romance novel scratches the itch. Your "inability" to be on time, showing up fifteen minutes late, could be your roundabout way of reminding yourself that you matter more than you let yourself believe.

Speak tenderly to your vices. Let your vices show you what they are. Scolding them or labeling them with a prepackaged term before they can actually be specific to you is a way of keeping yourself at bay.

What if your distractions are the socially acceptable shape of your creative power? If you were to merely remove them, you would feel the absence. But if you let them tell you about yourself, they can become your greatest authority. You don't need to be solved, even those parts of you that you really hate. The more you resent them, the more there is on the other side of that door.

UNDOING CONSISTENCY

Routines are lovely. Practices are beautiful. Habits really do lead to transformation. But aiming for consistency itself is a distraction.

For the vast majority of brilliant and creative humans I know, aiming for consistency as the end and the means does more harm than good, especially when it comes to creating something meaningful.

Here's why: consistency is superficial. It mistakes a symptom (showing up regularly) for a cause. It's necessarily externally focused, not internally derived.

Consistency asks, Did you do it or not? Did you do it often enough? It's all or nothing. Win/lose. Never mind that human growth and the creative process (which are not so different) are cyclical.

And as soon as you focus on the binary of doing or not doing, you're setting yourself up to find failure when reality throws you off. If you get sick, or your child needs you, or you learn something that changes your perspective, you might step back. But when consistency is king, those events are problems to fix as quickly as possible.

Even worse, when the focus is on doing or not doing, your relationship to that action that you *wanted* becomes transactional instead of intimate. It's about enough/not enough instead of being driven by love, or curiosity, or conviction.

In other words, when *doing the thing enough* is the goal, we change the meaning of the action.

Here's what I propose instead: our resistance to sameness is a feature, not a flaw. Our inconsistencies are golden places, holding valuable information about where we are and who we are.

What if there is a fallow period in every single process under the sun? What if stepping back (or falling back) is necessary? And I'm not talking about taking weekends off.

I'm talking about having such trust in every part of your process that you expect and welcome even the pauses and the endings.

Instead of asking yourself how you can do-enough-for-long-enough, what if you ask yourself how your curiosity about this "goal" can grow deeper? Or how you might deepen your conviction? Or your passion?

Internal motivations—passion, or curiosity, or conviction—also have ebbs and flows. I don't feel curious all the time—but I can bring curiosity to that lack of curiosity. I can say, "I'm getting bored with this, I wonder why?"

If inconsistency isn't a problem, then you won't punish yourself when everything in your body says "not today."

And if you're not punishing yourself, you won't spend all day feeling vaguely like a failure.

And if you haven't spent all day feeling vaguely like a failure, then you won't wake up the next day and decide, "Maybe this goal, this hope isn't for me. Maybe there's something wrong with me."

Does that sound familiar?

You can work out consistently because you're afraid if you don't, then you'll lose control. Or you can have a relationship with your body that is expressed and explored in movements.

When I started going to the gym regularly for the first time in my life, I went every day because I was afraid of how guilty I would feel if I didn't go. If I missed a day, I would think, "It's all over. Surely I am going to stop going altogether." The doing of going or not going was the only thing that mattered. I learned nothing about my body. I certainly didn't love my body any more no matter how toned it got.

Consistent action is a *by-product*—one of many expressions of an ongoing relationship between you and the world. The relationship could be between you and your body, you and your community, you and your creativity.

A painter I worked with came to me, initially hoping to figure out an ideal schedule for her studio time. She was afraid that if she did not figure that out, then the project would never move forward. I could tell by the way she was hoping for the schedule to solve her internal discomfort that she was worried about her relationship to her painting.

She told me she was afraid that if she did not establish a consistent practice now, the demands of her job and her parenting would take over forever. I asked her, "Do you think your creativity is going to leave you?" She started crying. "I'm afraid that I will give up. I will leave *it*." But it was obvious to me that her desire to paint was never going to go away. It was part of who she was; her creativity loved her back, as does the creativity in everyone. But she was trying to schedule the wedding when her relationship to her work in this new phase of her life wasn't ready for that.

If your creative capacity was a relationship, what would it need right now in this season of your life? Probably not the next six months scheduled.

When the painter stopped demanding an ideal consistent practice, it became obvious how to work painting into her actual life. She could see that what she needed was two hours a week to just noodle around in the studio without the pressure to make anything. After a couple weeks of that, she wanted to start gathering materials for a new series that was percolating in her mind.

She didn't need consistency, she needed curiosity about what her relationship to her painting needed in the moment. When she got her feet under her, and it was time to take on her new project, she was off and running, developing a regular practice after having taken a break for a year. What she wanted from "consistency" was the joyful flow we all want in our lives. Now she knows, if there is a season she can't make it into the studio, she can find her right pace by looking at her relationship to her work.

So when you notice you're at an "off" point in creating or in any transformational process, welcome it. It's a friend: a loving, long-term relationship. You don't measure the success of that relationship by whether you do the same things together all the time, or in the same ways.

You trust that it is there, allowing you to show up however you are. Even and especially when you're simply lying on the couch.

The paradox: when you stop pouring shame upon inaction, you're closer to acting on your values. You can speak to yourself with enough kindness that you can do difficult things that matter to you.

TERMS AND CONDITIONS

I could see my daughter as wholly perfect on the day she was born. I even joked about it to the nurse checking my vitals. "She will never make a mistake in her life!" The polite nod the nurse gave suggested that she didn't know if I was kidding, which made it funnier.

But the wholeness I saw her in threw a harsh light on how imperfect I believed myself to be. The way she needed me broke my heart for her. How could this perfect *being*, this pure and utterly lovable nugget of life, lay on *my* chest of all chests? Me, a blubbering, angry whirlwind of unfulfilled potential. A frequently petty, socially awkward, and desperately needy shrew of "advanced maternal age." That would not do as this cherub's mother. No, I clenched my jaw and silently decided I must protect her from all that me-ness. I determined to be a Not Bad Mother.

You see, I had read the popular books on parenting, attachment styles, and how trauma can pass down through generations. I expected myself to be the calm, confident Good parent to this Good child—a parent who was, at worst, occasionally frazzled in a cute, sitcom mom sort of way. I used this moral ideal to disguise my distrust in myself.

You could call this rejection my terms and conditions for being. It happens when we sign an invisible form full of qualifiers of who we can and cannot be before showing up in any creative capacity.

These were my specific terms and conditions for being with my daughter: I could love her and be her mother, but I must be Not Bad. Not Too Much of Anything. Just Right. Have you ever tried to be Not something? The mind does not respond well to negatives. It's like the cliché: Tell people not to think about a pink elephant and what will appear in their mind?

The way Carl Jung might put it, everything you reject in yourself and the world you shove into your shadow, where you can't see it but you can feel its presence; it does not go away because it's inconvenient. All the conditions on your presence live in this shadow like an overstuffed closet you have to keep pushing closed. If your personal terms are that you must be In Control, everything out of your control like illness and death will set up camp in this dark part of your mind, threatening to ruin you.

We think that if we don't put the terms and conditions on ourselves, we will screw everything up. Maybe if we stop focusing on Not Doing Bad Things, we will betray our deepest values. If your plain existence is clueless, lazy, unproductive, and twisted, you best do everything you can to keep yourself in check. Plus, you have to earn your keep to maintain any worth on the planet.

The qualifications are unspoken daily expectations we have learned to meet to justify our life. I am okay only if I guarantee everyone feels good at the end of the meeting. If I seem smart. If I keep the system chugging along. If I am profound. If I say "please" at the right time and don't overstay my welcome. If I'm in a great mood. If I'm not like the jerks we hate, the bad people with terrible opinions and poor taste.

To start from the premise that your mere existence, your plain showing up, your effortless breathing, your unposed form chilling out at your specific coordinates in the cosmos is wildly acceptable, well, that's a problem for business. You've signed no contract, checkmarked no user agreement.

115

Yet I could be with my baby only to the level I could be with myself exactly as I was. This was easy when I was in a good mood, because that was acceptable. But if anything, from a poor night's sleep to a spat with my husband, threatened my Not Harmful image of myself, I withdrew in shame. In my effort to protect my daughter from the worst of me, I showed up as a shell of me. What an alluring, impossible standard: to avoid the inevitable failure inherent in becoming who we are here to be.

Telling yourself what not to do keeps you out of a creative life because it places terms and conditions on your wholeness.

We are smart enough to know this on one level. The more we are preoccupied with what we must *not do*, the more we accidentally create the thing we're afraid of. It's like running straight into a brick wall because you're looking behind you.

That shows a fundamental distrust of your inner knowing. Your inner knowing has no terms and conditions for you. Your presence is enough, though your doing self struggles to comprehend this. No, your presence goes beyond enough, because enough and not enough are still measuring with old rulers. From the perspective of your inner knowing, you just *are*: whole.

What becomes available if your presence is all that is needed?

If there is nothing to prove or perform, a whole new field is available to play in: generosity, spontaneous insight, curiosity, and power.

I invite you to see how uncomfortable it still is for you without terms and conditions. It's terrible, actually. To the doing self, releasing your whole self from the edits of expectation feels like death. Because it is. The death of who we feel we must be precedes the life of who we really are.

UNDOING FIXING

"Her first feeling every morning was shame about all the things wrong in the world that she wasn't trying to fix." In my twenties, I circled this line from Sheila Heti's novel *How Should a Person Be?*, then copied it in my notebook to journal about. Sheila, the protagonist of the book, is an artist who questions what art-making is for. The author explains, "Sometimes she felt bad and confused that she had not gone into politics—which seemed more straightforwardly useful."[1]

A fixation on fixing, the one Sheila and I nurtured like an orchid, does not come from your inner knowing. Your inner knowing does not care about fixing. Noticing? Loving? True repair? Yes, absolutely. But inner knowing is not in the fixing business. Its imagination is bigger than that, and that's why your inner knowing can stand beside all the problems you are trying to solve without drowning.

The opposite of fixing is *being with*. When my heart was smashed after a particularly brutal breakup, a dear friend opened the door for me at midnight. We lived in the same building on the same floor, so on bad days we could walk down the hall wearing a blanket around our shoulders and knock on each other's apartment, knowing the door would open from the other side. Her "come on in" is what allowed me to stand up out of my defensive crouch, not the assurances that "he sucked anyway!" When days passed and it was time for me to get off the couch, she gently coaxed me to join her grocery shopping, brought me along to the gym and showed me how to use the machines. She could do this because she knew that I was not the experience I was in. She did not need to fix me.

As producers, we are reluctant to really *be with* ourselves as we are today because it seems like giving up on the self-improvement project we've been told to make out of our lives. Your producer self would much rather *do* something about it, "it" being the product of your life—fix it so it stops being a liability, a debt you'll inevitably pay.

But being *with* is not a nice addition to your life—it is a precondition for making. Presence makes real growth, not just "change," possible.

Being with is the opposite of fighting with reality—arguing with facts, with pain, with chaos, with joy, with bubbling, surprising truths that are a wee bit inconvenient. So when you drop the arguments that always start with "should," you begin to see beyond the blinders.

"I should not feel tired," so I will argue with myself that "I should have gone to bed earlier and they shouldn't have woken me up" and "I should not live in a society that does not afford me more freedom." You are tired. Being with that tiredness lets you see what kind of tired it is—before the imperative to fix busts in with violent solutions. Is it body-tired? Soul-tired? Thirsty-tired?

Being with means climbing out of the boxing ring where the problem lives. Being with means refusing to punish yourself for experiencing the problem. It means you stop agreeing to hate yourself until it's fixed.

Be with the part of you that does not want to be with yourself.

Your inner knowing's only agenda is to invite more truth, more reality, more of life into view. Then, possibility arises. This possibility feels obvious (if not always pleasant). It's like letting your eyes adjust to the dark and finding that maybe it's not pitch-black after all. Maybe there's enough moonlight for the next step.

UNDOING PRESSURE

As producers, our body associates pressure with being squeezed into painful, inhuman shapes: The One Responsible for Your Brother's Tantrums, The Machine Who Diffuses Customer Complaints, the Pleasantness Generator Who Turns the Aching Balloon of Guilt into a Grateful Smile and Fear into a Smooth Solution.

In the land of productivity, it's not obvious how to discern the difference between the pressure imposed by a machine, or by systems of punishment, and the natural pressure that moves babies through the birth canal or holds bridges together over the river.

When pressure is only a punishment or external mechanism of control, we producers run from it, obey its demands, or collapse when we feel it coming. We treat it as alien to our systems, because since most of us were children, we've experienced painful, forceful pressure from the outside, telling us how to survive.

My first year in college was a shock, to find myself in classrooms full of intense, type-A achievers who carried around heavy books and, even worse, read them. I dropped out after my first year.

After having pushed myself to meet external expectations throughout high school, it was understandable that I would hit my limit, though I didn't understand why it was happening at the time. All I knew was that I preferred to work at a video store where the only expectation was to fetch the videotape from the back shelf and give it to the customer. Then I made lattes at a coffee shop and sandwiches at a bakery.

My inner knowing wanted to create something else, but I couldn't discern the internal pressure of creativity from the productivity pressure of the outer world. I needed to change the external demands at first. There is a time for shifting the demands; then there is a time for changing your relationship with demands themselves.

Choosing safe containers of expectation was the beginning of getting my creative feet under me. I volunteered at an art gallery. I offered to do photo shoots for free for local bands. My inner knowing led me to the stress I could handle without harming myself.

To run from all pressure is to run from all desire, all dreams, all consequential acts. All that's left is wishing, waiting, or immediately releasing what you were too afraid to hold like a hot potato.

You are a powerful force of nature, capable of working with the stress and counter-stress that creates balletic leaps and the heat that builds and seals the jar filled with strawberry jam. You are not separate from that strength.

Your role as a maker is to seek the loving consent within you to hold creative pressure with safe presence, as your inner knowing intends. If you do not, you will project all pressure outside of you, seeing it as a threat. You will call everyone else the problem—the source of your demands.

The truth is, the life growing in you will create pressure whether you like it or not. Running from responsibility is its own kind of pressure. If you find pressure is ambient, like a shrill repeating strain of elevator Muzak following you from room to room, that's how you know you believe your very being is at stake in your performance. It is not—not anymore.

Maybe when you were a child, the pressure to perform was associated with love, which is security, which is belonging. You resent this, which is why you run from it now. You were right to do so.

Before leading a retreat group for the first time, I stalled and hemmed and hawed, toying with reasons why I wasn't the right one for the job. What if I failed them? What if I froze and/or made a mistake that hurt everyone's feelings? In my mind, I pictured responsibility as a heavy burden . . . to prove that I was worthy of the heavy burden.

Now, as a maker, you redefine how to work with pressure. You turn the old story that pressure is the price of earning love into a tool: you can stay with pressure and work with it. You skillfully apply it to forge weapons of truth, goodness, and beauty. You let it move through you to birth small revolutions in your bedroom. I'm not saying that we all need to submit to or welcome every pressure that arrives. Only that as producers, we will only be able to see pressures as incoming judgments on our performance, but as makers we can see them as facts to respond to, or not.

A maker works with pressure like a blacksmith uses fire. If you see a deadline as an incoming judgment on your worth, then it looks like a threat. But if the deadline is completely neutral, a wall that you toss a tennis ball against, then your experience of it is very different. Then it becomes possible to choose your own pressures, like setting goals for yourself, or asking your friends to hold you accountable.

Some fellow writers have asked me how becoming a mother affected my creativity, as if the all-consuming demands of parenting might have crowded out my creative life. While of course there is tension between these competing demands—and many an op-ed has been written about the difficulty of "having it all"—for me, the responsibility to care for another burned away a lot of distracting pressures I'd placed on myself, all the frittering and self-protection that got in the way of my inner knowing. I just didn't have time anymore for wanting to impress the people I used to want to impress. I didn't have time to avoid discomfort. That constraint was a freedom.

Maybe you want to start a newsletter. You allow the self-imposed weekly pace to be a practice in expressing without preciousness or perfectionism. Maybe you can let yourself be a leader in your family, your community, your work, turning the old pressure to please everyone into the freedom to embody your values and bring others along.

UNDOING THE CAN-DO ATTITUDE

If you're asked on a date and you can't say no without being harassed, that's not a romantic request, that's a threat. In the same way, it is impossible for you to say yes to meaningful action without the freedom to say no. Your inner knowing might really want to take up painting, go trail running, speak your mind in the meetings, or block off Saturdays for connecting with your people, but you cannot force it. Your resistance to action, even acting on your deepest values and desires, must be honored.

What if it's true that you absolutely cannot act on your best intentions today? Or at least, some hefty resistance within you says absolutely not, no matter how much you put it on the schedule and try to convince yourself it's what you want.

Much traditional self-help pathologizes this resistance, calling it "staying in your comfort zone" or "settling for the old you." But resistance is not merely "self-sabotage" or "fear," it indicates the presence of another agenda, a different desire competing with your conscious intentions.

In an electrical circuit, resistance represents the measure of opposition to the current's flow. It generates heat and light, which we use for electric heaters and the light from light bulbs. Within your resistance lies heat and light. It is a kind of oppositional intelligence.

In a poetic twist, this electrical resistance is measured in ohms, symbolized by the Greek letter omega (Ω), which means "the end." And what is a story with all beginnings and no endings? An interminable bore.

The part of you that wants to act on your brilliant ideas and best-laid plans is a ravenous and optimistic cheerleader. It belongs, in its buoyant way. You might admire its vision in the face of a world that says you should just try to maintain what you have.

Yet if you feel so much pressure to live the Good Life, the life with all the markers of joy and abundance, to the exclusion of everything that is not that, I invite you to seriously imagine giving up. (I know; this is motivational sacrilege, but stay with me.)

You might say, "I want to pursue this possibility that is nagging at me, but I can't. I want to expand, but it's so hard."

Then why do it? I'm serious. Can't you give up?

"But I can't give up the idea; I would feel unsatisfied."

Okay, what if you felt unsatisfied?

"Then my life would be miserable."

How would it be different than how you feel now?

"I still have the potential to do it now."

Yes, and how does that potential feel?

"Like guilt. Also safe. But bad."

Exactly. So you know how to feel bad; putting "giving up" on the table just opens up your options. Allow yourself to picture and really *feel into* what it would be like to never, ever do what you're feeling guilty for not doing, even the most ideal, life-giving actions.

Even if they seem wonderful, moral, and even convenient for you in the long run.

What if you never crossed off a bucket list item, never made a painting, and left your draft as a draft forever?

What if you just continued on living exactly as you are now?

I don't say this to scare you into action—quite the opposite. If you feel false guilt about not doing what you desire to do, you are convinced that there is only one right choice you are failing to make. Yet your resistance is digging in its heels, saying, "Get that expectation away from me. I am fine as I am."

And your resistance is right. You are fine as you are. There is no looming failing grade coming for you even if you never become everything you want to become. Where you sit this minute and every minute going forward, in your very being, you are perfectly beloved.

All the while, underneath that pressure and fear that you must act on all good impulses is your innate energy, capability, and deeper desire. But you can't feel it when you're shouting, "You should be doing this."

Letting yourself imagine giving up is the first step to reclaiming your sovereignty from the pressure to produce the best of you. It's reminding you that you do have a choice, even if every choice looks terrible from where you stand.

To insist on "overcoming" resistance at all costs traps you in your beautiful dreams and desires. You can let them go. Until it is safe to let them go, it's not safe to pursue them.

If you do not have a choice, you might half show up just to tell yourself you tried. Or you could negotiate with your dream, saying, "I'll do it in the smallest way, just so you get off my back."

So consider this your Imagine Giving Up Challenge.

Your first reaction may be some form of fear. Sit with that long enough to let it settle. This fear is telling you it's life or death, it would be *intolerable* not to do the thing, so you *must*.

And indeed, it might be heartbreaking to imagine giving up. But until you get out from under the "you must or else" pressure, you can't really show up to your "yes."

That heartbreak is pointing you to what you value. Therein lies your natural, creative love.

UNDOING PUNISHMENT

Are you afraid of failure, or are you afraid of how you'll punish yourself if you fail?

You swore that this time would be different, but it wasn't. It would not, in fact, be the year you ran the half-marathon, or even the week you jogged around the block. You set your alarm to get up early and meditate, but you hit the snooze and scrolled on your phone instead.

You read the book that would keep you from snapping at your partner for leaving the garbage overflowing, again. And you succeeded! You kept your mouth shut right up until you saw the towel crumpled on the bathroom floor. You set out to paint a masterpiece, a profound expression of your soul, but after months of labor, you give it a C−.

Production land believes you must apply force. If you are what you do, then punishment for your bad doing is always justified. A suitable correction for you, the producer, is required. This punishment program creates two options in you: use force to "fix" yourself, or run away from the threat.

So when you make the rules, and inevitably disobey them, you hide from yourself and from your intention. You pretend you never said you would, or try to forget it. Or refuse to try too hard again.

That's the way the punishment program frames your productivity. It's not so different from the spirit within the so-called justice system in the United States, seen on the walls of a California parole office: "Trail 'em, Surveil 'em, Nail 'em, and Jail 'em." In other words, you watch and wait until something goes wrong, then punish yourself.

These are the secret threats you have been taught were "motivation":

Do it or you will go broke.

Do it or you will lose love.

Do it or you will be a loser.

Do it or you will have to give up forever.

Do not do it or you will prove them right.

Do not do it or everyone will suffer.

Do not do it or they will leave you.

Do not do it or everyone will see what you're really like.

From diet culture to the prison industrial complex, the punishment program doesn't just hand out demerits but rewards too. You justify eating your own birthday cake because "I've been so good this week" or "I worked out so I deserve this"—as if you need to earn your joy and nourishment. There are Good Points to even out Bad Points. With a good deed, "I can cheaply purchase a delicious self-approval," a Wall Street employer in a famous Herman Melville story says. It "will cost me little or nothing, while I lay up in my soul what will eventually prove a sweet morsel for my conscience."[1] Goodness can work as currency for paying off psychic debts.

When you forget your being—that you exceed anything you could do—you use the logic of punishment to set yourself (and others) straight. But it can never go deep enough, because this punishment is an attempt at inappropriate controlling action, forcing a deed upon ourselves or another to "level out" a past deed. I didn't paint enough yesterday (arbitrary "bad" action), so now I'm going to paint extra hard today (arbitrary "good" action).

Punishment is always a tool of control. If you can get someone to fear punishment, then you can get them to stop listening to their inner knowing. And if you can get them to stop listening to their inner knowing, then you can get them addicted to fixing themselves.

And if you can get someone to be addicted to fixing themselves, then it's very easy to sell them solutions and profit from their seeking.

If we ask ourselves what to do from living inside the punishment and reward program, our inner knowing will be conspicuously quiet. Your inner knowing does not wield carrots or sticks. Your inner knowing does not punish or mete out gold stars because it looks at you through the eyes of innocence.

You may remember the old folktale by Hans Christian Anderson that tells the story of an emperor who loved fine clothes above all else, and who famously wound up nude. Allow me to remind you of the details.

One day, two con men arrived, claiming they could weave the most beautiful fabrics imaginable. These clothes also had magic: they were invisible to anyone who was either stupid or not fit for their position.

The emperor, excited by this promise, paid the swindlers a lot of money to begin weaving. As the swindlers set up empty looms and pretended to work, the emperor sent officials to check on their progress. None wanted to admit they could not see the fabric, so they all nodded and clapped at the fake creations.

Finally, the swindlers announced that the emperor's new clothes were ready. They mimed dressing him, and the emperor pretended to be amazed by the clothes' beauty as he set off in a procession before the whole city. The townsfolk, having heard about the fabric's magic, also didn't dare to admit what their eyes could plainly see. They all cheered and praised the emperor's fine clothes, until a child, innocent and honest, shouted, "But he isn't wearing anything at all!"

The crowd knew that the child was right, but no one dared to say it. The emperor, however, continued the procession, naked and prouder than ever, as his courtiers held up the train of his pretend garments.

Regimes of punishment mess with our minds. No matter how cloaked or indirect the threats, they shape the way we think.

Recent neuroscience has shown that the punishment/reward centers in our brain are strongly activated by value judgments, by the perceived "rightness or wrongness" of our actions. These punishment/reward centers helped our evolutionary ancestors find food and avoid harm. They are very deep. They have been found in creatures like sea slugs.

Because they are tightly wound with the ancient parts of our brain that help ensure our survival, the mechanisms that make us hyperresponsive to judgments from ourselves and others have a powerful hold on us. This has often kept us from being harmed by egomaniacal rulers. We have sometimes needed to fall in line with one regime or another just to survive.

But there is always a part of us, like the child in the fable, that escapes this kind of regime.

Like the child, your inner knowing has nothing to prove or disprove. He can tell the truth and set everyone free. Inner knowing reveals the innocence (that which does not injure or harm) that sits outside the realm of punishment.

A maker knows that the alternative to punishment is not reward but more connection. When something has gone off the rails, there's been a disconnection within you. From there, you can ask this vast self, "How are you really? What do you need?"

The answer will be of a much higher quality than the question "What should I do to make up for what went wrong?"

From the eyes of your inner knowing, actions are just an expression of one part of your vast self. Because you are not equivalent to what you do, you are free to choose your next steps based on new parameters.

Maybe the answer is a walk and a truth you need to see between the branches of the trees. Maybe it's a break and a phone call.

UNDOING DISCIPLINE

You may believe you lack discipline, that it's the missing ingredient between you and the abundant life. Yet even if you long for discipline, you resist her. In productivity land, this push-pull with discipline keeps you in thrall to your doing and not-doing.

The way I hear about her from my clients, discipline is punishment's prim partner. Sometimes she appears as a buttoned-up, sexless scold in shoulder pads, tsk-tsking at any squishy capacity for commitment. She worships deprivation and going "all in" on a program for six-pack abs by summer. She'll be the first to forgo extra guacamole and strike lattes from the budget when the money gets tight because small indulgences—she's very concerned with "extras"—are her domain for control.

She's a secular ascetic, accruing moral capital with all the strictness of a desert monk, without the aim for heaven. Heaven on earth with discipline means warding off the chaos for another day.

You must be honest about her productive appeal. She can be seductive in her intimidating way. She takes cold showers at five in the morning, and her skin glows from the benefits. She *loves* green smoothies. She is so *composed*. She draws straight, satisfying lines.

The word *discipline* is Latin in origin, likely arising from the earlier "disciple" and containing a cluster of meanings around learning and following.

Under the emperor Hadrian, the word took on special importance on the Roman frontier, where it was associated with obedience, duty, and especially faithfulness to the customs and beliefs of the imperial center in Rome.

Discipline was so valuable that a minor deity known as Disciplina, perhaps invented by Hadrian himself, appears during this time as an object of worship.[1] Evidence related to the goddess has turned up at various fringes of the empire, at Hadrian's Wall in Britain as well as in North Africa. Soldiers revered her for her virtuous balance of frugality, sternness, and faithfulness to their unit and the empire.

The further out you went from the center of power, the more useful reminders of where you had come from—what you were a disciple of—became. The soldiers needed to constantly remind themselves they were not like *those guys*, non-Romans.

So much so that it became useful to worship the idea of discipline itself, the act of remaining devoted when the object of one's devotion was far away.

It has remained a favorite religion in military life. The motto of the US Marines is *semper fidelis*, always faithful. But it is a religion familiar to most of us.

You may have the urge to be disciplined—that is, to become a disciple of an intention you set, some core value or way of living.

If you drift far enough away from the heart of that value or lose sight of your vision, you may soldier on, worshiping discipline itself.

To merely desire to "be disciplined," to worship discipline itself, is a desire to subject myself to correction for its own sake. Maybe this has its uses. But I would much prefer to be a disciple of what is alive in me, to "stick to it" by following a thread of something: learning, or life, or intention.

We are all disciples of something, though not necessarily on purpose. Everyone is studying some corner of the world closely. Perhaps it's how to make more money. It could be the bottom scroll on CNN or the fantasy of being a perfect partner. Maybe you're the accidental disciple of your family's moods. Or you faithfully watch fantasy dramas into the wee hours because, in reality, you are a disciple of epic romance, longing to live romantically in your daily life. What is it you gaze at with rapt attention and form yourself in the shape of?

When discipline is on its productive, moral pedestal, whether you're chasing it or fleeing it, you cannot see what you are *really* the disciple of.

What do you do when you believe you are *not* disciplined? I picture any and all activities we put under "laziness." Lackadaisical scrolling, being sloppy with your time, money, and belongings. When you think you aren't disciplined, that you must fight against yourself to acquire it, you forget your power as a maker.

I can see the times when I have been the most meaningfully disciplined; I kept my nose close to my subject. I let myself be formed in the shape of my loving attention. I said yes to being an eternal-student-of instead of a master-over.

UNDOING SENTIMENTALITY

My undergraduate college required students in my department to take a certain number of studio art credits, but I did not want to get my hands or clothes dirty every day. I was hung up on getting through school as quickly and efficiently as possible, so that ruled out pottery, painting, screen printing. All the fun stuff. I signed up for the classes that let me sit at a desk or in front of a computer. By keeping my hands clean that year, I kept myself safe and pretty much the same.

You will be freer to make meaning when you stop avoiding the fray, staying out of the mess. That is, when you're free from the need to be sentimental.

Sentimentality is characterized by the one-dimensional thinking born from your doing self's desire to be *not that*. You can spot sentimentality by its precious neatness. Think Hallmark movies where the ugly anger, mixed motives, and awkward phrases are conveniently deleted. Think also of cable news networks whose expert talking heads smooth our daily history into a story of winners and losers. In a sentimental world, only bad people do bad things and good things only come from the actions of heroes.

Your inner knowing is deeply tender but not sentimental. Sentimentality does not work when you're making a creative life because it makes you precious. It has you worried about wrinkling your pants and dirtying your boots. It holds you back from finding renewal in your shadowy parts. It keeps you on the sidelines of life, which makes your world small.

Your inner knowing is willing to let stories end without all the threads tied up neatly. It does not need to keep making sequels and reboots until you're finally the hero.

Our inner knowing will simply not let us make our days into scrapbook pages for very long. It's exhausting.

When I studied with nuns at a Benedictine monastery, most of our readings and conversations aimed at helping us *unlearn* sentimental ideals about prayer that got in the way of real intimacy with the divine. It's hard to feel spiritually alive when prayer is a series of polite and persuasive noises recited to an uptight, omnipotent judge. "In prayer we say who in fact we are," write psychologists Ann and Barry Ulanov, "not who we should be, nor who we wish we were, but who we are."[1] And who we are is both bitter and sweet. We brake for geese waddling across the road while hoping the driver who cut us off in traffic spills coffee on their lap.

Sentimentality undermines a creative life to the degree that it resists reality. Sentimentality has you thinking, "I need to go back to when it was easier," "I need to fix this so everything feels fine before I move on," or "I can't go there because then I might compromise the image I have of myself as *this* kind of person."

If your inner knowing has gone silent and your inspiration has flown away, it might be because production land paints in black and white—good guys and bad guys. And producing to be sure we are the "good" guy keeps us very busy.

There is conventional wisdom out there in parts of the wellness world (which I consider myself a part of) that insists on "purity" to a fault. This purity has the neatness of sentimentality. There is a chain of value that links moral cleanliness to bodily immaculateness to the inherent goodness of nature. Think of any number of organic food brand slogans: "As good as nature intended it."

This makes our internal landscape—which is endlessly complex—a mere vehicle for the old Romantic myth of nature, that it is only gentle and harmless, a representation of simple goodness that stands against the smog and pollution of industrialized cities. But you are a force of nature and you are not only gentle and harmless.

If there's a part of you that yearns to create, to express, to do more than maintain, then you're a villain as much as you are a hero. Your "victim" is the deadening norms of production land, the status quo that resists imagination and real engagement with the mud of material reality.

As a villain, you question the received "I have tos" and draw closer to the landscape of what is.

Accepting that you are also a villain might draw raised eyebrows, nitpicking criticism, and the feeling of isolation—but it also brings authenticity and the freedom to jump in instead of keeping your hands clean.

You are both sincere and playing it up a little. You are alternately deeply self-interested and justice-minded. You are soft, warm, and capable of great mayhem. Embrace this combination, and you unlock a storehouse of energy that was spent smoothing out your proverbial dress.

All your work to ensure a neat ending is unnecessary.

PERHAPS

If the doing model needs to be certain, our inner knowing says "perhaps" to our false certainties. This releases us from the pressure to do—or run away from doing—things the way they have always been done.

"I can't believe you didn't submit your taxes. You're so lazy."
Perhaps.
"Everyone will make fun of you."
Perhaps.
"You must be excellent."
Perhaps.
The great thing about "perhaps" is that it does not argue so much as shrug.

"Perhaps" was one of Irish author Samuel Beckett's favorite words; in his plays he saw danger in tidy conclusions, takeaways, "neat identifications" of all sorts, preferring the elemental human creativity of what was unfinished, beginning again and again. "Will it not soon be the end? I'm afraid it will. Pah! You'll make up another."[1]

We say "perhaps" to outcomes, "perhaps" to results, "perhaps" to failure, "perhaps" to success. We say "perhaps" to pressure. We say "perhaps" to our own treasured opinions.

Perhaps dissolves our false predictions.

Imagine a friend played you a song they wrote, but before you could say a word, they interjected:

"You probably think it's too weird. No—let me guess. You think the lyrics should be more political. The bridge is probably your favorite part."

You would be rightfully annoyed, thinking, "Give me a chance." Their projections would be distracting from your true response.

I do a version of this sometimes when I think my neighbors judge me for leaving the empty garbage can at the curb for hours instead of dragging it back into the garage promptly after the trash collectors have arrived.

"Tsk tsk." I put the thoughts in their head every week. "What a lazy, thoughtless woman."

It's an old habit—the way I pretend I know what these lovely people think about me, or that they're thinking about me at all. It is my ineffective mind reading of life. Of course, like any maladaptive habit, it worked well at some point. Predicting social responses is how we often learn what's expected of us.

Creatively, though, it's a killer. Mind reading is the first thing that happens before we filter our inner knowing into something less shining and honest. Every time we cling to what we are certain will happen or what someone else is thinking, we dilute our inner knowing.

Your inner knowing is capable of replacing the habit of prediction with an active unknowing. This goes further than curiosity.

Allow yourself to take on a deliberate fogginess where there was once a predictive point of view. There's one rule: no assumptions. Whenever you are tempted to write someone else's line in your head, you can inwardly shrug.

Your producer self might hiss, "Ooh, so-and-so will think this is so dumb."

"Perhaps!" your inner knowing replies. "That's not for me to say."

Your producer self offers, "That outfit is too much for those people."

"It's possible?" your inner knowing says. "But that is none of my business."

Once we shoo away the phantom judgments of the future, we hear our own wisdom more clearly.

We can ask, "If I had no idea what others would say and no outcome was determined, what would I see? What would I want? What would I think? What would I do?"

UNDOING FALSE GUILT

Do you feel guilty about not working or are you just being different than you've expected yourself to be for your whole life? Your inner knowing does not feel guilty about not being productive.

Productivity guilt is false guilt, because doing for its own sake—the definition of productivity—is not something your inner knowing values.

If we choose to act from our inner knowing over external stress, if we choose to change the expectations for our own actions from doing, doing, doing to being the makers we are, we're also going to have to accept other people's reactions to that.

In the same way it feels risky to freely eat a cookie in front of your family of chronic dieters, it might seem rude to be the only one taking a few days to text back without apologizing or making up excuses.

The land of productivity is a social program, so if we opt out, the problem glitches on everyone around us too. Similarly, if we opt out, it catches on.

Should we decline the invitation to perform the habitual role of our doing self who allows everyone else to say their favorite lines and strike their usual poses, there will be a conspicuously empty seat at the table.

If you have always been the person to fill gaps and check off boxes for others, you're going to get a reaction. Your doing self is going to want to fix that, but your maker self can hold the discomfort of false guilt.

What we call productivity guilt is really false guilt—the discomfort of going against the cultural pressure to associate an outcome with your worth. Maybe you chose rest, and you feel what you think is guilt but it's actually just the discomfort of making a nonconformist choice from your being.

What you might call guilt is possibly the discomfort of bringing something to life through the stages where it looks like nothing tangible is happening.

If you feel "guilt" for spending time making a slow meal for yourself instead of a nutritional smoothie, that's not guilt. That's the discomfort of choosing beauty over function.

From the perspective of your inner knowing, the closest feeling to guilt is not judgment or punishment. It's a painful twinge that arises when you're consciously betraying who you really are. Put another way, it's when your outer actions and your inner knowing are incongruent.

The feeling of incongruence from our inner knowing is specific to a situation, not a wholesale judgment on who you are. It's a gift calling for your attention. I feel it when I say yes when I mean no, or no when I mean yes.

A maker knows that dead ends are not a mistake, so there is no reason to feel guilty about spending hours on something that didn't work. That is just the discomfort of being in a longer process than your calendar expected. You as the maker will feel discomfort over not knowing how many hours it will take to finish a painting, or the discomfort of waiting for that breakthrough on a particular knotty math problem. That discomfort is not guilt.

When you choose your values over false guilt, you are creating a new reality. For yourself and for others.

NUMBNESS

We supposedly civilized grown-ups are frightfully well-tamed. Look at us stand in line for coffee and tsk the ill-mannered jerks who would dare take too much time ordering. Watch as we hesitate to tell the barber not to cut the back of our hair too short.

While the definition of "polite" shape-shifts between cultures, classes, and places, we learn our version dutifully by the time we are adults. We go through the proper channels. We keep things moving at the speed of business. We live in a *society*, after all.

But too often the price we pay for our obedience is secret rage: bottled passion that is hidden from our view for being inconvenient.

In Dante's *Inferno*, the medieval poet's vision of hell, lazy souls are condemned beside too-angry souls. They're submerged in the Styx, a putrid swamp. Their punishment is to stay eternally stuck in this filthy water while remaining as they are, too uncaring to lift a finger or make a move. They get the extreme of what they wished for—the monotony of not caring forever.

By contrast, the wrathful souls, fueled by uncontrollable rage and fury, are always itching for a fight. They go at each other like rabid animals, biting and tearing into flesh with an insatiable hunger for violence. The "slothful" ones live in the cross fire, absorbing the explosive outbursts of the wrathful, because Dante knew this: the "lazy" are also angry. The slothful and the angry aren't plain opposites but inversions of each other. The sluggish souls are not calm, they are passionate about blocking their inner fire.

If you feel uninspired or numb, you are kinking the hose on your anger. Your anger is what passion feels like when it's been ignored too long. If there's no safety valve for anger, it can look like low-grade resentment, a commitment to indecisiveness, and "accidentally" starting arguments or getting hooked on drama that isn't yours.

To the philosopher Paul Tillich is ascribed the adage "Boredom is rage spread thin." Inspiration will not move through sludge.

A producer thinks that if she feels anger, she will have to act on every harsh thought that comes with it. But anger is not a thought or an action but first a sensation. Your inner knowing is strong enough to stand beside that fire and work with its heat.

In her essay "The Uses of Anger," the writer Audre Lorde describes how the sensation is an appropriate, creative tool against racism. "It has served me as fire in the ice zone of uncomprehending eyes of white women who see in my experience and the experience of my people only new reasons for fear or guilt."[1]

For months postpartum, I was furious at everything. The traffic, my body, the microwave's beep, and every minute I had to wait for my husband to come home from work. Hormones, of course, and lack of sleep will do that. But that "logical" explanation did nothing to quell the deeper need my carbonated rage was trying to show me: the thirst for more connection and support. The kind that communities over millennia have known was necessary and that no extra naps could quell.

Only a moment's curiosity could have shown me this, if I had not been so busy trying to not be angry. This anger, too, is a form of love. Its "no" to the current state of affairs bubbles up from a deeper "yes" to what is possible.

UNDOING REGRETS

Nothing will snuff out the imagination faster than sneering at yourself for what you haven't done in the past. The way you treat the actions and performance of your past self not only inhibits the actions of your present self, but unless it's changed, it will be the exact same way that your future self treats what you do today.

The reason that forgiveness for your past self is so important is that you will hold back from doing anything risky from your deepest values if you anticipate the condemnation of your future self if it doesn't go well. If you're saying, "I should've started earlier" or "I can't believe how stupid I was," that anger and regret is what you're trying to avoid in the moment. And we know that actions based on avoidance only create another version of what is feared.

Only creative acts, done from a free intention instead of trying to outrun a negative reaction, create new meaning, new life.

What story do you tell about the life you've lived already? Specifically, how do you evaluate the choices made, those that failed and those that succeeded?

As a maker, you look at both wins and losses with understanding, though not in an abstract way that needs a label for every experience. You do not need to have the perfect psychoanalytical understanding of your attachment style or the personality defects that see you act in certain ways. I mean the understanding that comes from a deep curiosity about how it made sense that you did what you did. How it made perfect sense based on a holistic review: of the culture around you, the information you had at the time, the fears that were operative, and the best-case scenarios you could spot on the horizon.

If you treat the mistakes of your past with tender care and reverence, you can trust that future-you will treat present-you with the same respect. If you look back on your journals and cringe and push them away, then you will convince yourself that your best efforts now are just waiting to be thrown away.

It's not so much the popular phrase "if you know better then you do better," but when you can love who you were better, you can love infinitely more than you thought you could now.

Being creative instead of merely productive means cultivating a nurturing, loving relationship to who we are, who we were, and who we could be, without condition.

You were fully human then, you are fully human now, and you will be fully human in the future. There is nothing to run from.

BEING WITH OTHERS

The productivity model thrives on isolated parts.

When we believe we are what we do, then we think we are responsible for making our very selves—that our life is a product to project manage. The pressure to produce tells us we are alone in all our doing; that it's all up to us. In a disenchanted, mechanistic world where the results are all that matter, isolating parts is more efficient.

We treat ourselves the same way, as a collection of interchangeable, isolated parts, as if our lives are portfolios of assets we can invest in or hedge against.

Our inner knowing says otherwise, and our bodies tell the story of integrated wholeness. Our brain's mirror neurons come alive when we watch another person feeling something, as if we're experiencing it ourselves. They infuse us with empathic seeing, letting us understand the world from the inside out.

Consider that in any given forest, the trees are talking to each other. Their roots intertwine like underground fingers, forming intricate networks that breathe life into the soil. Through these hidden channels, trees exchange nutrients, whispers, and warnings.

Scientists call them mycorrhizal networks. The roots team with specialized fungi, extending their reach beyond what they could achieve alone. These fungi act as loyal messengers, delivering nutrients and chemical signals from tree to tree. When danger strikes, a tree in distress releases a chemical cry for help. Through the network, neighboring trees receive the message, readying themselves against the imminent threat.

A maker knows we are not isolated actors. We are collaborations, made up of history, the earth, time, and each other. We become who we are in the presence of others.

Maybe you never felt consistent presence from others. A lot of us didn't. But I bet you had it in moments where a friend laughed at your joke, when a teacher helped you up without a word, when a cat brushed up against your leg, or a baby stared shamelessly into your eyes. A pat on the knee. "You do not need to do anything for me to see you. You are welcome without condition." Such belonging is the fundamental truth of the universe, and the deadliest weapon against the lies of unbelonging wielded against all creation.

The poet Peter Campion once told me, "If undergraduate writing isn't good, it's because they haven't been listened to yet." In other words, a lot of what we call "bad writing" happens when a writer is shouting because they don't expect an attentive audience. If you haven't been listened to deeply, you probably won't speak with subtlety or sincerity. You might exaggerate or say the easier thing. You could reach for recognizable (but tired) phrases to get your point across. The truest part of what you want to say will get lost in the noise because the truth best emerges, especially at first, under hospitable conditions.

The role of a maker is to listen to yourself and the world around you. Maybe that sounds like a passive act, as if you're a bored but tolerant psychoanalyst nodding while a patient discusses her dreams. A more apt metaphor is this: you're sitting in a boat, holding one end of a delicate line in the water. On the other end is a heavy, flailing fish: the truth trying to climb up out of the water into the air with you. You mustn't yank the line, or it might break. You hold it steady and watch. You can't drop your end.

In other words, we listen each other into greater being. It's not a demanding interrogation that asks, "What do you *really* mean?" It's curious but relaxed. Our soul is drawn out like a cat under the bed who will not be rushed. Sometimes it's not even people who do this for us, but nature, or the awareness of being heard in prayer and meditation.

When I first moved to the US at twenty-seven, I was freshly heartbroken, in the middle of deconstructing and reconstructing my whole philosophical worldview, and my sister got very, very sick. I found myself in the middle of a story I didn't ask to be in, when the old scripts would no longer do. Something new in me had to emerge, but that's hard to find alone.

At the same time, I found myself in the company of friends who listened, who could hear the person I was becoming through all that uncertainty. I hope I did the same for them. They did not give me ten rules for surviving your late twenties in a new country. Instead, we stayed up late talking. We made each other meals. We were honest when we were hurt. We met at dive bars with peanut shells on the floor and made amends.

Their listening told me I was real—even when I struggled to believe it myself. Listening will surprise us that way; then we find ourselves more curious to listen in return. Maybe every generative act, indeed every act of love, is really saying, "You truly exist." That belief can give us the courage to look more closely at reality.

UNDOING IMPOSTER SYNDROME

Every single maker I know is a maker precisely because of what they struggled with, not in spite of it. I regret to inform you that the exact quality you think might disqualify you from expressing your deepest values is your ticket to ride that ride.

"I am so emotional; no one will take me seriously." "I'm too shy for this." "I don't look like the people who are doing this already." "I'm not experienced enough." "No one cares about what I care about." "I struggle too much with anxiety."

In the land of production, our particularities are liabilities. A producer has to hide half of her humanity. And if you feel vulnerable, production land can convince you to produce faster and shout "I *do* belong here" over your sneaking suspicion that the rooms you find yourself in were not made for you.

The answer to imposter syndrome isn't simply to overcome that doubt and insist to yourself that you really do belong, but instead to transmute that doubt into the self-knowledge that will restore your deep sense of internal validity.

Our most creative acts come from the meeting of our love and our wounds. We make the most meaning around what we struggle with. Pain and struggle have a gravity that keeps us orbiting around the wound. Our pain pushes us to find insight and solutions. We become experts on our greatest source of confusion. I've seen it time and again—what we help others with is where we are the most tender. Then, where we are the most tender becomes how we help others.

If you've ever thought about someone else, "Because you exist, I feel more free," chances are good that this person has done the work of undoing some imposterhood. Chances are they have looked at what might make them inauthentic or unwelcome, transmuted it into a source of their own inherent authenticity, because they sat with and deeply registered a part of themselves that was a core source of pain or shame. They used their sense of difference as an occasion to truly *know* one of the deepest and most complex parts of themselves.

That knowing now speaks to you as a source of welcome.

Figure out exactly what you feel like an imposter about: What are you scrambling with all your productivity to avoid revealing? Is it that you're an experimental musician from a small town where no one listens to anything but country? Is it that you're a gentle soul living in the city where everyone shouts?

Your so-called weaknesses, your vulnerabilities, that made you feel that you are an imposter, are what is needed to dissolve the barriers of shame that hold you and others back.

As theologian Henri Nouwen wrote, "Shared pain is no longer paralyzing but mobilizing, when understood as a way to liberation."[1]

You are that which is needed. You are a maker. A maker can never be an imposter because a maker's presence creates belonging for others.

BEING IN-BETWEEN

You cannot turn yourself on like a switch. You will need to get used to warming up to reality, to responsibility, every day. The production mindset sees this as a problem to solve. All of us have within us a truth to be expressed, a response to the world, waiting to be nurtured like a child. And like a child, it needs to be approached softly, with curiosity, and coaxed into full presence.

It's not easy to shift out of responding to emails and putting out metaphorical fires—the day-to-day reactive fixes that we are invited into—into creative action, whether it's a walk to clear your head or journaling or using your imagination. You are not shifting tasks but shifting states.

Even if you keep your center, moving from one state of attention into another will involve resistance. We always forget this, and we make it mean that we are incapable. This is a function of the forgetting, of seeing ourselves as high-maintenance robots and not evolving life-forms. Stop expecting the transitions between states to be smooth. When you can accept that, that the resistance is not only normal but on some cosmic level necessary, then it has much less weight.

If that sounds infantile or inefficient, a reminder that you shouldn't need to hear, that would make sense, because we've been taught to treat our minds like computers. The computer model of the brain is a popular way of imagining our psyche: you plug in to the right power source—your food and sleep—then apply pressure to the switch of your willpower and go. The metaphors for technology infiltrate our imaginations of the soul.

If you have a day job that invites you into production mode and you expect yourself to shift into your deeper identity of a maker after spending eight hours as a producer, you're setting yourself up for disappointment and frustration. You can shift on purpose by welcoming how awkward it feels to move your body fluently after being on high alert all day. The hardest part is the beginning—that liminal space between states.

Your muscles are stiff after sleeping, and it's your role to wake them up gently. A maker inhabits the thresholds in your life as they are, in the knowledge that they are necessary and not an accident, but also impermanent. Too often we make our creaky muscles mean that we are a stiff person. We bring it into our identity. "I am bad at this because it's uncomfortable." No, you're just waking up, and soon you'll be awake and in the flow.

You will forget occasionally about your creative capacity for all kinds of reasons. Sometimes you will forget it because you've gotten caught up in external demands or a crisis and you're putting out fires.

Sometimes you might forget first thing in the morning as your half-conscious mind starts counting the obligations and controlling for their outcomes. This is not a mistake; forgetting is part of your process, remembering who you are as a maker. When you notice that you have forgotten, just laugh. Smile at your grogginess.

There are reliable times of day when it can happen. The witching hour before dinnertime, the wee hours in the morning. When the sun is making herself known, we wake up to how we've been.

Artists throughout history and athletes have warm-up exercises. Why should we expect that we would be any different as we

152

focus our energy onto being-driven acts after living in a producing world? Move your resistance through you on purpose, like clearing your throat, and let yourself hear your garbage thoughts before you expect yourself to say anything brilliant. Imagine six impossible things before breakfast.

BEING IN RITUAL

The abundance of books about the routines of famous people suggests that we have a fascination with rituals. From their inner knowing and not their doing, a maker gets to create their own.

Ritual technology has been used for centuries to facilitate transformation and transitions—from the sacred to the mundane. We use rituals to welcome creative presence: a comfy chair, a cup of tea, a marking of the time. Because inner knowing begins in our body, our knowing likes the body to greet it; it appreciates the warm welcome.

It's not so much that ritual guarantees a result but that you get to set the table with your body to say, "I want to be with this, whatever is happening." When you say "such-and-such helps me focus," you might expand that to a less utilitarian approach—one that is more devotional than disciplined—independent of your mood.

Rituals at their best honor our fragile relationship to time by marking it clearly and respectfully. As if to say, now is the time I am present with my meal, my children, my writing, my emails. While the land of productivity values a "seamless experience," ritual is a visible seam. It stands against the endless scroll, the one-click-away, the work-from-the-beach, the constantly available life.

Rituals may seem frivolous, like adornments on "real life"—a waste of time. But we know how much the veneer of seamlessness costs—how disappearing our waste does not make it disappear at all. That's an illusion. How much psychic energy it costs to switch from tab to tab, from a meeting on one screen to an email on another, to a notification on the phone. It's the invisibility of those transitions that increases the drag. Of course, the land of productivity wants it to remain invisible, so we internalize the difficulty of transitions as a moral problem, a "motivation" problem, but humans are meant to be present. It is our healthiest state, and rituals are formal ceremonies of presence.

Of course, the rituals can harden into mere doing, another rote set of actions, but that is when they are not allowed to be present themselves.

When rituals are forced into mere doing—defined by action over intention—they are not allowed to die, so they cannot be alive. Rituals are not static—though some last millennia, others may last a week. The length of time doesn't determine how *real* they are. Some rituals remain, but you must leave them for a time to become present with them again.

LISTENING TO SILENCE

When I am too full of the noise, my thoughts get dull and repetitive. I feel both flooded and empty, uninspired. I regress to the most bratty version of my teenage self, standing in front of my bursting closet complaining, "I have nothing to wear!"

To step outside your productive self, you must create your own silence. You need the dark side of your mind like a painter needs a canvas to paint on.

As a producer, you try to do enough to earn it. The silence that you crave is an end to the urgency and expectations of others.

Even as you think silence will give you the peace that you know belongs to your being, you run from it because you don't know who you are—unless you are telling yourself by your actions or bolstering your importance with information.

You must find a way to incorporate silence into the noise instead of trying to control what the noise is saying.

You can arrange your life to avoid the noise, but you cannot ever do enough to find silence outside of you.

The Unabomber, Ted Kaczynski, tried to flee the modern world of technology because he believed the noises, the mere existence of other people, to be an impingement on his freedom. He built a remote cabin as far from civilization as he could find, and still the writings that the FBI found after they arrested him for his murderous bombing spree revealed his fury at the grind of the regional sawmill and the planes flying overhead. You can never run far enough from your mind.

The practical producer is the one whose mind is filled with all the data that could be used to maximize their life. But just like a jazz musician knows the notes resonate in the space between the music and a poet would tell you that meanings often arise from what isn't said, you must create inner and outer spaces for your soul to absorb the meaning you're already making.

You might have resistance to this, because you think that no space can be created. You might even say that it is a privilege to find silence because not everyone on the earth can afford a seven-day meditation retreat. But silence isn't just an absence of noise, it's a posture of attention with the body.

You can create silence by imagining yourself covered in a thick wad of cotton between the urgency, the subway announcements, and the calls for a meeting in ten minutes. It's the conscious separation of your being from the stimulation, and the willingness to be in that gap.

The attention economy will do what it can to capture your inner world. You have to be willing to not know things, as knowing is not the same thing as wisdom.

A maker does not need to fill every gap in time or conversation because a maker is listening instead of thinking about what's next. A maker connects through empty spaces as much as through content.

It's funny, the way silence connects you through disconnection; it lets your doing-thinking-planning self remember she is not alone. It adds texture and adds punctuation to time.

A maker will fill his body with silence. He is willing to leave the party, to go for a walk in between meetings, to feel his footsteps on the ground, to slow down his response.

This silence is risky. You might not have seen the latest movie or have the fastest quip. You will see how others react in the gap of

157

your speech or your presence in ways that you might not expect. You will hear yourself think and say things you don't expect.

Even so, the risk of living without silence is the cost we pay by living productive lives: to be half asleep, only hearing half the truth, seeing half the goodness, and making half the beauty that's available to us.

As stillness practices like meditation and prayer tend to show us, you will notice more sensations in your body that you were too busy doing over to find.

You must also sit in the discomfort that you will never do silence enough, because that's the way it is with infinite things. This makes us not want to do it at all; this makes us not want to put ourselves in the way of it. Don't be precious about it. If you wake up early to watch the sunrise for eight minutes every day, or turn your phone off, don't let it be an achievement. Don't let it become another obligation that you need to uphold.

Think of it as an experience that you're giving yourself, like a meal. It comes and it goes; it nourishes you as you carry it with you in your body. The taste of silence is different every day. Some days it will be bitter like gas station coffee. Other days it will be blissful, and you will look forward to when you can have seconds or thirds.

BOREDOM

Boredom is not the blunt discomfort that has you flipping channels, scrolling real estate listings for homes you'll never buy, or looking up ex-girlfriends just to "see what they're up to." These behaviors are the daily flight from boredom, which in its repetitive trance becomes a new mundane task.

In production land, boredom can trigger a fight-or-flight response since, in its flatness, it feels as if you're not moving forward with all your doing. You think you need to do something about boredom to make it go away.

And the productive world is deeply boring with faux urgency, the way standing in a security line at the airport is boring. It's not simply a lack of stimulation; it's urgent flatness. Boredom shows you the same thing over and over and asks you to believe it is equally important every time. This is how the productive world manufactures boredom: by limiting how much and how deeply we can pay attention.

We cover our boredom with stress because that makes it feel more important. We deny our boredom, maybe because we think it means we are weak or boring ourselves. Children, on the other hand, have no problem throwing their heads back in despair and announcing their state. My three-year-old will ask for the next episode of *Mr. Rogers'* before the first one has finished.

Every kind of boredom is a signal that some form of life is being ignored somewhere. This is why boredom is a portal for the maker that must be passed through like a dark hallway. In boredom, the contents of our consciousness shuffle into our awareness. While the producer's impulse may be to flee from boredom through distracted behaviors, the maker recognizes this awakening as the great gift of boredom.

If you are numb and bored, admit it. Let the sensation rise to the surface.

Getting this intimate with boredom is as brave as remembering your mortality. When your mind can't latch on to anything, you feel cut off, which feels like the death of all your striving. You are being "bored to death."

Entertainment will not solve boredom but only make it worse. The amusing diversions from reality, the ping-pong table or cereal dispenser in the office, keep you trapped. This fun without stakes cannot scratch the deeper itch.

In *The Need for Roots*, the philosopher Simone Weil knew this: "Risk is an essential need of the soul. The absence of risk produces a kind of boredom which paralyses in a different way from fear, but almost as much."[1]

On a Sunday night in my twenties, I joined a group of folks who had just come back from partying at a local music festival at the local dive. An acquaintance turned to me as we lingered around the bar and said, "I don't even know why I'm here right now. I've been out all weekend." The words escaped my mouth before I could catch them: "Because you're afraid to be with your own thoughts?" He looked at me with both recognition and horror, mumbled something under his breath, grabbed his shot of tequila, and walked away.

A risk of boredom is that you notice what is inconvenient to notice.

Just after my thirtieth birthday, a milestone that threatens you with the expectation that you should already have arrived at perfect stability and "adulthood," I went on a trip with my kind, handsome, totally-wrong-for-me boyfriend and his friends. While I was stuck in a cabin in the Adirondacks with no wifi and no work to do, it became obvious that our relationship had run its course without our busy Brooklyn routine. After a tense train ride back into the city, we broke up within a week.

Risk how boredom will show you where you are living and where you are not. The risk is not that you will ruin your life, ending relationships that are meant to last and quitting your job to move to Paris. It's just as likely that you will donate old clothes, paint your bedroom, or call your grandmother.

When you let boredom undo the false urgency to produce, making can begin.

PART III

MAKING

How to Bring
Your Inner World
to the Outer World

INVENTING CREATIVITY

It doesn't matter whether you use the word *artist* or *creative* to describe yourself or not, or whether the idea of creativity conjures a professional wearing fashionable glasses, a divinely inspired solitary artist, a kid covered in finger paint, or something else entirely.

I define creativity as cooperating with reality to draw out more life. This is a serious act—holy and practical play. When we stop cooperating, we sit out of the game. And we wonder why we're not having any fun.

Productivity is doing for its own sake—acting *on* the world. Creativity reflects the fact that the life in you is in a reciprocal relationship with the life outside you. So rather than asking what to *do*, a maker asks what spark of life is inside them, asking to reach into the world.

It makes sense if this sounds unfamiliar. In the land of productivity, the term "creativity" lacks teeth. Its everyday meaning lies somewhere between "hobbies to distract you from real life" and "commercially viable novelty." It's one of those words that *sounds* really meaningful, but when you look at the kinds of activities it is often actually associated with, it appears flimsy.

When I tell people that I write and teach about creativity, I wonder if they imagine me professionally encouraging grown adults to take up macaroni art or tree-house decoration.

Or maybe they think I'm helping corporations exploit people more easily. The creative potential of people is "the ultimate resource," says venture capitalist Marc Andreesen's recent "Techno-Optimist Manifesto."[1]

Some have argued that the modern concept of creativity is an invention to soothe the workers in a postindustrial society, to assure them that they are not replaceable cogs in a machine, inputs in an algorithm. "Look how *creative* we expect you to be with your presentations, with your time, with your own schedule. You're not a frustrated employee; you're a rebel! A true maverick at your whiteboard." To celebrate creativity in all its vagueness soothes the anxieties of our capitalist, Western mind.

How did it get this way?

In the "Doing Deep Effort" chapter, I explained how the verb "create" originated in the Middle Ages as an already-completed action which was performed by God, as in various existing facts (planets, nature, and so on) that God had brought into being from nothing, something that was simultaneously timeless and utterly new.

This meaning was fairly quickly transferred to certain kinds of "god-like" human activity, especially to artists, and since then it has been gradually further democratized. After being extended to certain privileged humans, beginning in the nineteenth century and culminating in our own day, creativity has come to be seen as part of the birthright of all humans.

Before the Renaissance, in Europe "artist" was a broad term, denoting something like "having skill in making." Once it became strongly associated with the idea of god-like creativity during the Renaissance and culminating in the era of the Romantics, however, "artist" became associated with the heroic, solitary genius working in a few select "fine" arts. He (they assumed the artist would be male) was responsible for capturing high feeling, meaning, and beauty, primarily for elite consumption.

The artist was "a more comprehensive soul, than are supposed to be common among mankind," the Romantic poet William

Wordsworth wrote, "delighting to contemplate similar volitions and passions as manifested in the goings-on of the Universe, and habitually impelled to create them where he does not find them."[2]

By the mid-nineteenth century, people like the critic Matthew Arnold had taken issue with this version of creativity, arguing that creativity extended well beyond the realm of solitary genius and fine art as such, pointing out that "if it were not so, all but a very few men would be shut out from the true happiness of all men."[3]

Creativity was an important part of individual ethics, in other words; it was something that should be accessible to all as part of a full life.

In the late nineteenth century, the designer, writer, and activist William Morris sought to democratize the idea of creativity further, criticizing the schism between fine art, the province of the elite, and working-class and peasant "craft," a division he saw as one of the chief mechanisms undergirding the capitalist cultural order.

This trend of democratization has continued to today, with both life-giving and unhappy results. What has become democratic is not necessarily the role of artist as such, which still retains many of its elite connotations, but the main property artists possess, creativity.

This has been particularly true in the workplace. "If you think creativity is only for artists," the US Bureau of Labor Statistics noted in 2018, "think again."

Luc Boltanski and Eve Chiapello suggest that since roughly the 1960s, management styles in Western corporations have tended to view employees as "self-organized, creative beings," as opposed to the earlier form of workplace administration that viewed them in a somewhat mechanistic way, through the lens of the specific tasks they performed.[4]

A good shift, with some downsides. A "creative" workforce is easily made into a workforce of quasi-entrepreneurs, an army of gig workers who "would really prefer not to be traditional employees." Creative beings are often assumed to be willing to work at their passions harder, longer, and for less pay.

We may overlook more fundamental problems with the culture and economy if we believe, at least, that it frees us to pursue creative self-fulfillment. "You're not an unfulfilled worker; you're a nonconformist at your desk."

The result of all of this gradual democratizing and the entry of creativity into the market has been twofold. On the one hand, the land of productivity has harnessed our creative potential as a new natural resource to exploit, a new "essence" that offers a seemingly endless source of value for the market.

On the other hand, though, since the nineteenth century and increasing dramatically now in the twenty-first, more and more people are aware that they *do* in fact have powerful, creative essences within them, parts of themselves that can be shaped and harnessed by others but which are, at the end of the day, truly their own.

More and more of us have become curious about how we can know this creative dimension of ourselves better and get to know it independent of external control.

In other words, the history of creativity in the land of productivity has led us to a unique place where we can see a path *out* of creativity-for-production's-sake. One that's always existed in one form or another. This is a path that is not fixed by the whims of market forces or paved with old stereotypes, but a road lit by our inner knowing. This inner knowing transcends mere doing and becomes a way of creative living I call "making."

Moving from passive consumers or frantic producers into collaborators, we shift creativity out of its role as a resource, or commodity captured by the market outside our control, and into a daily practice that we own.

A BURNING SPARK

To be a human is to have a divine spark of life within you to tend, nurture, and apply transformative effort. If you ignore it, throw it down the stairs into the basement of your consciousness, it will burn your house down.

I briefly dated a semifamous musician, a rising star who flamed out, leaving articles written about his mysterious absence from the scene in his wake. Dating him was like being a tornado chaser—tracking the unpredictable movements from up-close-but-not-too-close for the thrill, while risking having my life tossed in the air. It didn't last long, but it lasted long enough for me to see that my desire to be close to him was really a desire to be my own force of nature. At the time, I was keeping my writing in notebooks and playing the Good Employee at my magazine job. I didn't want to be with him; I wanted the creative power that I was denying in myself.

He was running from his own creative capacity as well and letting it burn his life down, while I felt tempted to warm myself on that flame.

According to the Gospel of Thomas, Jesus says, "If you bring forth what is within you, what you bring forth will save you. If you do not bring forth what is within you, what you do not bring forth will destroy you."[1]

There is a cost to abandoning the spark of life within. This flame to make meaning within you is not benign. The cruelest people are those who abandoned their inner spark. You can find them becoming professional nitpickers, gossip-spreaders, code-pendents, tyrants to themselves and others. Thwarted dreamers fill the comment section under any given article with "Well, actually."

This isn't to say that everyone who expresses themselves becomes self-actualized, losing all their hang-ups through their work. If that were true, we could all take improv classes instead of seeing a therapist.

The problem comes when we set our inner spark against the rest of our life—when we make a real desire, an image of what's possible, a problem to manage or repress. I'm picturing the stereotype of the tortured artist who rages against everyday needs like groceries and sleep, as though regular life and the inner spark for meaning are enemies.

Once you get a nudge to make something, it's not your job to control it but to be a midwife for it.

You have to trust that spark of inspiration within you belongs in the world, so this involves some trust in the world, even when—especially when—it is bleak. You have to bring it forth, even if you have decided no one is ready for it. As a maker, you play with living fire at the beginning, the middle, and the end of your process.

Your creative spark will outgrow the comfort of your mind, as it should. It is as if your creative energy sprouts legs. If this spark gathers enough energy and you try to control it, to build a fence to keep perfect track of it, it will dig up the yard. At a certain point, when you have nurtured your inspiration well enough and not before, you must open the gate and set it free to roam, to seek others, to love, and to be loved. It must run where it runs, forming relationships, breeding more creation.

When inspiration reaches a point of development where it's ready to take form, free it from the comfort and privacy of your mind (or drafts, or safe little circle) for it to flourish. Until it becomes intimate with the wider world, it will be restless.

MAKING INTIMACY

The instructor of my first university art class asked each student in the circle why we showed up. "I just love to smear paint around," said a long-haired girl with a shrug. Her answer earned an approving nod from the instructor, but I couldn't understand why. Her reason didn't seem very . . . reasonable.

We spent hours staring at the same foot-long coil of rope in that class. If you had asked me what the rope looked like at the start of the assignment to draw it in detail, I would have said "yellow." By the end of the three weeks we spent on this one assignment, I could describe the dozens of narrow strings in each braided chunk, the buttery shade turning ivory at the two frayed ends, and the wonky way it looped on itself in the middle. It appeared in my dreams. My eyes began to see a dignity in it, almost a personality.

I did not ask to become familiar with an inert plastic rope, but intimacy is both the cost and reward of a creative life. Intimacy, the willingness to see and be seen, is a kind of devotion—not to an act, a title, or a status, but to the dirt, breath, and blood that make up the world.

As botanist Robin Wall Kimmerer wrote in *Braiding Sweetgrass*, "I've never met an ecologist who came to the field for the love of data or for the wonder of a p-value. These are just ways we have of crossing the species boundary, of slipping off our human skin, of wearing fins or feathers or foliage, trying to know others as fully as we can."[1]

A maker is driven by love. Sometimes, at its worst, it's a distorted love, distracted love, all twisted with anxiety and control. But the maker is a lover first.

A maker grows a close relationship with a tiny slice of life—an idea, a need, one place, one thing, to bring out more life.

Everything beautiful you have ever done has come out of some form of love.

You don't make friends to ensure someone picks you up from the airport, no matter how nice that would be. You text, make plans, and show up to experience connection, to laugh at their jokes, and to meet another's eyes across the table.

In the same way, a maker's efforts are not for a convenient result but for intimacy between the self and the world.

If your relationship to your work, paid or not, was a relationship to a person, what kind of relationship would it be? If you were watching it on a screen, would you call it codependent, fraught, adoring, or estranged?

Your work is not you. You are in a living dynamic with the material of life, so ask yourself: What is the quality of that dance?

To be intimate with your efforts means you have to deliberately reach out to the world and let the process change you.

MAKING INTENTIONALLY

As Alice finds herself in Wonderland, she asks the Cheshire Cat which direction she should go. The Cat replies that it depends on where she wants to get to, but she doesn't know; she only knows it is *somewhere*. "Oh, you're sure to do that," assured the Cat, "if you only walk long enough."

Your action and inaction will surely get you somewhere, if only because you live in linear time. But a maker does not simply choose a direction, she *intends*.

It used to confuse me, at the beginning of a yoga class, when the teacher suggested we set an intention. Standing on my mat and suddenly aware of my crumpled posture, my brain would search itself for a goal or wish: *What am I supposed to be doing here? Yoga just seems like a good thing to do . . . But that doesn't sound good enough. How about "presence"? Okay, my intention is "presence," whatever that means.*

"Intention" comes from the Latin *intendere*, meaning "turn one's attention" or literally "stretch out, extend." Most of us are not taught to take the magic of our attention very seriously—even though it is the resource that every technology conglomerate aims to capitalize on.

But it is magic. Intention is the invisible way you extend yourself toward a new way of being. What new story, new connection, new shade of reality, new shade of you, is all your effort for? The answer will be specific to you, particular to the moment.

Intentions differ from goals, but the difference can be subtle. Making a film because you want the end product is a goal. Naming the meaning of the story to you, *connecting* with it, for the purpose of sharing, is an intention. Goals are fine, but intentions give them life.

One maker's intention for her own healing was to be *really, truly in her body*. Another maker's intention for his work was simply *delight*.

I might dwell on the nourishment I want my family to feel when I cook them dinner instead of worrying about whether the rice will be soggy.

An intention might sound like a fluffy wish for a nice feeling or hope for an outcome. But to intend is to pray in earnest, to cast a spell. The Lord's Prayer declares a list of intentions: "Thy kingdom come. Thy will be done on earth as it is in heaven." The Arabic greeting "salam alaykum" calls peace upon another. We wish each other happy birthday, and when we mean it, it matters.

A producer often gets distracted by the *hows* when you feel a desire for action. "I've never made a podcast before, so how do I use the recording software?" You have endless choices in the marketplace, but you find that you cannot reduce your decisions to marketplace choices or best strategies.

Just as often the blockage is about the outcome: Will this be sufficient? Will my boss like it? Will it earn me a paycheck? Those questions keep us inside of ourselves.

But intention shifts your gaze. Your intention helps you slip past the *how*, past the bad infinity of the marketplace, past the boss, past the habitual self-consciousness that blocks your presence.

Think about intentions in terms of qualities in a world that asks for quantities. What way of being matters here? For my local coffee shop, I can tell the intention is to welcome. The music volume is just-so, and the baristas move as if they're in their own living room, in the best way. For one maker I know, his music always intends *fun*. Even when the subject matter is heavy, fireworks light up my mind as the lyrics bounce over the beats. He *embodies* fun, so his efforts *give this fun away*.

If you're selling a slice of pie, what do you want to give the other person besides a full belly? Do you want them to experience your delicate attention to detail or a surprising combination of flavors?

These are basic questions; they might sound almost too fundamental, because they *are* fundamental. Even as a child, couldn't you feel the difference when someone gave you a gift because they wanted to avoid disappointing you versus a gift given as an expression of their attention?

What are your intentions for yourself in the process? What do you hope to learn, to experience in all your efforts? What would make showing up worth it for you if you released the result as an offering? Sincerely stretch your attention toward this possibility and see what magic unfolds.

IT'S NOT ABOUT YOU

You have become intimate with the seed of an idea arising from the life inside you, and you have an intention to share it with the world. You are experiencing what is generally meant by "inspiration." You feel this life breathing in you, through you, toward others.

As soon as you notice that, you might notice an equal and opposite force that blocks this breath, a voice that tells you to stop, that you can't do it, it will cost you too much, plus it's embarrassing and it's been done before. You try to encourage yourself by telling yourself that you can do it and inflating your own confidence.

Meanwhile, the opposing voice is insistent that you can't. You sit in the center of a can-and-can't binary. This looks like being stuck with neglected potential, a half-baked draft of an idea that you haven't so much said goodbye to as already abandoned out of shame. You can sometimes hype yourself up, but when you do it from the doing self, the fuel burns out quickly.

Your inspiration is not about you. So while you can hear all day that you can do it, that you are good enough, until you see that your inspiration is fundamentally only evidence of your connection with the world, the collective human experience, you will stay pinned between Can and Can't.

"But no one else will care about what I see." The fact that you feel drawn to a possibility is evidence that it is needed. Ask for no further proof.

You didn't invent your inspiration, you received it. Whether you see the source as the collective unconscious, God, the Holy Spirit, cultural vibes, the zeitgeist, inspiration is not a piece of property but a public well.

It's through you but not about you. It's for others, but it does not belong to others.

My mother recently shared a secret she learned from her research with musicians. She is a retired music professor who studied vocal breakthroughs—those "aha" moments when a singer could do what they previously couldn't do, like stretch their range or sing a long strain of notes in one breath.

It turns out self-consciousness blocks a breakthrough. For a singer, self-consciousness might look like monitoring the tone of their voice and trying to replicate the "right" sounds.

Instead, if the singer focused on the shared meaning of the words, their body could create what it had never created before. Thinking beyond themselves set the singer free to expand.[1]

If someone sees their partner as a reflection of how cool and worthy they are, not as a person in their own right, they cannot freely love. It's the same with our efforts. We cannot make our efforts into a thing whose purpose is to reflect how capable or incapable we are. Well, we can, but we won't make much meaning from it. The more we think about ourselves and how we meet or don't meet a received standard, the farther we are from the purpose.

In other words, focusing on where your actions *point outside of you* is more powerful than getting hung up on whether you're doing it "right." Connection—not correctness—creates momentum.

MAKING IT "GOOD"

"I haven't written anything good in months," a musician told me at the start of our coaching session. "I can only get so far into the song," he added, "then I just hate what I've written." That day, instead of arguing with his vicious inner critic that his work was, in fact, good, I turned the problem upside down. His assignment for the week was to write the worst song he could muster. "Really lay it on thick," I said. "Turn your ambition in the other direction. Don't just write an okay song; go all the way with the 'awfulness,' whatever that means." After some protests that he didn't have the time, that this silly task would interfere with his client work, he agreed.

He returned the next week laughing. His begrudging experiment in doing it all wrong found him plonking on the xylophone, rhyming about bears, and generally having a blast. He would never share it with the public, but that wasn't the point. He let himself use sounds he hadn't played with in years. He remembered his sense of humor in the process—a quality that he used to include in his professional work but that got lost along the way. What was supposed to be a terrible song reminded him of what was more useful than good—what was alive. Isn't that what we're looking for when we aim to get it "right"?

Unlike the productive pressure to fill the predetermined quota, a maker defines a new version of "good" with their efforts. A maker sets the terms, because the regime of "ends" and "returns" is at odds with the discovery of what's true.

You do not know whether what you make will be any good or not. The truth is, you can't know what you mean by good yet, but you are sorely tempted to guess because you desire a return on investment for your time. Too often this desire has you holding back, playing it cool before you begin because you're not sure it will be good. This guarantees that it cannot be good, because you haven't started. Do not play it cool.

Or you stop in the middle because you think it will not be good, because the relationship is awkward and you see all your floppy sentences and wilted efforts that don't match the hope in your mind.

Or you hide your finished work because you anticipate the audience will not deem it good. Perhaps you've already mentally brought the audience into your space, let them witness your fumbling attempts to court your creative self, and asked them to pass judgment.

And then what? And what about the worst-case scenario, when you finally bring your creative intimacies forth into the world and they fail? Who will you be then? Only products and objects can really suffer from failing a standard, not a maker. A maker has always gained from the process.

When in doubt, what makes our efforts *good* is the same thing that makes for a really good date: aliveness. That won't arise because someone used the smoothest lines and brought you to the right restaurants. It happens when someone arrives ready to lock eyes across the table, respectfully and playfully responding to the moment.

I invite you to look at the goodness standard itself and ask, whose is it? How will you know when it's been reached; does it touch you, move you, disclose anything about what you specifically know to be good, true, and beautiful? Maybe a failed work is only a work that hasn't been made fully alive yet.

MAKING WITH THE FEAR OF FAILURE

Most of us makers are dragging around an old fear of failure. You keep trying to shake it off, since it slows you down. Instead of leaving the house to start that community garden, write your novel, or meet the love of your life, you stay put and mentally search the premises for the solution to the fear. With this *thing* hanging around, you can never quite do more than maintain.

You wish the fear of failure would just go away, so you give yourself pep talks about overcoming it. But you cannot make much without facing what failure means to you. It has a benevolent message underneath.

There are two kinds of failure that a maker faces in the land of productivity. The first is the way we "fail" to show up, even and especially to our own desires. You can call it failure-in-advance. It looks like the withdrawal, or the half-hearted attempt, at being in your life. You say "No, I couldn't possibly" out of habit, bury yourself in busywork while complaining about it, and become an expert in other people's dramas instead of writing your own story.

It feels like carrying a nagging weight of unfulfilled potential, quietly growing heavy with envy and regret. This is as much a result of the pressure to produce as it is a rejection of it. The fear wouldn't hold any water if you did not believe that your identity depended on what you did or didn't do: the volume, the quality, the recognition of having done.

Trust me, I have spent years failing to try lest I do it badly, making *me* bad, which at times has led me to become extremely critical of anyone who dared step out on a limb. This is an almost universal occurrence; the degree to which you cringe at others correlates to how much of yourself you cringe at.

One day after a beer or two, I moved out of the audience onto a stage at open mic night to sing two mediocre folk songs with my autoharp. I blushed and muddled my way through, proud it happened and relieved it was over. As I took my seat, my friend, a professional musician quipped, "It's not so easy, is it?" I never had more respect for him—the humility it takes to be seen trying without a productive purpose.

The second sort of failure is the obvious kind; we know it when we flop. You find yourself deflated when you open the rejection letter, swing and miss, get fired, dumped, or canceled.

This includes the sneakier mini-rejections that so often go un-witnessed, yet we turn them over in our minds: the way we were snubbed at the party, the unanswered texts, unliked social media posts, the promotions given to someone else.

Parts of the self-help industry and the land of productivity talk a big game about overcoming the fear of failure to encourage you to *do*. The mantra "fail fast" became popular in the world of computer systems and start-ups to encourage innovation and speedy greatness. Their idea is to discover what *doesn't work* early so you can find what *does*. Get the failure over with so you can get to the success part.

In my conversations with makers wrestling with failure—whether it's failure-in-advance or after it's happened—we've sat with it long enough to see that resistance to failure is actually resistance to the idea that anyone or any circumstance will stop us from bringing forth what's within us. In other words, we think failure means the game is over. What we wanted to make isn't for us after all. But for a maker, making is never over. It's an endless way of being.

A maker fails best when they make as if the worst has already happened. Fail as if you have already failed so there is nothing left but your naked heart. Don't merely "dance as if nobody's watching," dance as if you have already become a viral meme for your unusual moves. Love as if you've recovered from a dozen heartbreaks, so what's one more?

MAKING ABUNDANCE

Puttering around my sewing space, I fretted over wasting fabric. I started piecing one project together, then switched lanes before cutting into any fabric. I changed my mind over and over again about what to make, so I committed to nothing. I ironed. I mended an older piece.

My doing self told me, "Danger! You might run out of fabric, or time, or energy. Make sure you know what you're doing before you commit so it's done correctly."

It is so interesting that my doing self knew that throwing "waste" at me would stop me in my tracks. It sounds like such a mature thought, though it's really a lie about scarcity in fancy clothes. It appeals to a false sense of prudence and morality.

Waste fabric? How, by using it? I have piles and piles of fabric in my studio. Most of it is thrifted, some of it I bought over the years. If you stepped in that mess, you'd find linen of varying quality, heavy ivory canvas, stretchy jersey, old cotton bedsheets, small squares of silk, wool from salvaged blazers, denim from jeans that don't fit, polyester-blend XXL men's button-up shirts in warm tones that I love, and who knows what else. I'm not exactly working with priceless artifacts.

All that unused stuff I've hoarded for this exact purpose, and there I was, afraid to make a real piece out of it. I tell myself the same thing with wasting ideas, or time. And where does that belief in waste lead me? Into puttering around, "wasting" time and ideas.

When I trust scarcity, I create waste. In production land, we'll do this by default because we're surrounded by fake urgency, lies about lacking, and billionaires who couldn't possibly let themselves be taxed lest that slow them down from shooting themselves into space.

A maker practices believing the opposite on purpose. Ideas don't run out. When you use one, three more appear. Creative energy is not like crude oil, violently extracted after being formed over millions of years; it is like dandelion seeds emptying the seedhead and flying off to grow elsewhere at the slightest breeze.

The fact that creative scarcity is a lie doesn't just suggest that you go and make all the things either. It also means that you don't have to act on every idea, because another will come along. You don't have to frantically grasp, then despair if you can't bring it to life. A maker does not hoard it; you must either play with it or let it go.

Your mind is too precious to hold stagnating reserves of potential. More will come; the creative energy coursing through the world renews every morning. The more you make from your inner knowing, the more you have to make with.

As a maker, you learn the difference between living with abundance and having enough. As a producer, you thought that if you calculated your resources in advance, you would secure your needs. It has been easier for you to withdraw and calculate what support you might get before acting from your inner knowing.

Now you are learning that you do not know how to calculate your resources accurately because you are not God's accountant. You are learning to spend the best of you instead of saving it until you can guarantee a return.

A would-be community organizer may know only three people, a painter might have just four colors on their palette, and a scientist might be constrained by the current technology. These limitations are the stuff of reality. But makers look at the world in more than three dimensions. They do not deny the reality of limitation, they just add an "and" to the end.

You don't ask or act outside the bounds of what's been done before unless you risk saying "it's possible." It's possible that you won't always be an enemy to those guys. It's possible you can be paid for the way you love spending your time. It's possible there's more to your relationship with your brother than you can see right now.

Inviting this possibility does open the door to disappointment, but a maker can afford to be disappointed. A maker lets all the sensations move through him.

Everything your inner knowing wants to do is a kind of participation. Everyone who has gone before you is participating in your planting, the people who look like competition are evidence of what's possible, even your need, the emptiness, that you were trying to fill with your doing is proof of your deep capacity to receive.

A maker always learns that he does not know where the bottom of his abundance is. You are learning that the granary of love does not run dry. Your love, the same love that passes from the fish to the water to the riverbanks, which is also the divine love that makes leaves so green, and then also lets them fall, returns to you.

MAKING WITH GURUS AND ENEMIES

A maker is wary of self-proclaimed gurus. A maker has teachers, practices of devotion, and lineages to honor and respect, but does not see the teacher as the source of their improvement or a representation of what they don't have.

A producer will try to produce her growth by projecting all of the best qualities she can imagine onto a priest, expert, or influencer. She must set aside her understanding for the advice of a "higher authority"; she must disown her inner knowing in order to expedite the end result.

But as Walt Whitman put it in "Song of Myself," "every atom belonging to me as good belongs to you."[1]

A maker knows that a quality they see in another lives in their own shared treasury, including the capacity for all kinds of nonsense.

You are as brilliant and beautiful as your heroes and as ignorant and annoying as the person you least like at your dinner party. To believe we could never be like "them" is very convenient, but that underestimates how vast and strange we all are under the right light.

Do not say, "At least I'm not like them," or "I wish I could be like them." Hold a mirror in the space between you.

Adulation, pity, jealousy are very uncreative attitudes. They narrow your imagination for what is possible in a person or part of the world while exaggerating the distance between you and the world, destroying bridges between you and others.

And it's not an accident that comparison and conflict are hard-wired into us when we go to create something new, even in private.

The roots are deep in the Western world's social history, where models for making have always been shot through with psychologies of oppression.

In the history of suppression and co-optation of Black art by the white art world in American history, for instance, the novelist and poet Ishmael Reed found the germ of American art in general: "a rivalry between the oppressor and the oppressed, with a secret understanding that the oppressor shall always prevail and make off with the prizes, no matter how inferior his art."[2]

Describing the brutality of the still-racially-segregated writing world in 1970, Reed saw this history of brutalization as having far-reaching implications, suggesting that "here in America writing is related to bullfighting, or to sports in which men disfigure other men or animals—or sometimes it is compared to wreaking sexual vengeance upon a woman."

In addition to direct forms of social brutality that can still be found here and there, there's an atmosphere of interpersonal conflict in parts of society devoted to "creativity" that is frequently cutthroat and suppressive, and which rings out from this history. If you've spent time anywhere near workshops or seminars devoted to art-making, you've seen it.

Reed contrasted the oppressive model of writing to ancient forms like those of the Mayans and ancient Egyptians, in which "the writer [was] a necromancer, soothsayer, priest, prophet . . . who opened doors to the divine."

The point is not that we should all become necromancers or soothsayers, but that the psychology of making we have inherited, with all its me versus you, is not a given. It's just one option. There are others.

A maker can be promiscuously inspired.

An inspired life can't decide in advance what part of life is worth paying attention to. While it would be very convenient to block out large portions of the world as bereft of meaning for you, that is the most efficient way to become dull and uninspired.

The people you think you can learn nothing from represent a part of your own humanity that you're not quite connected with yet.

Make your own inspiration by listening to music you've never understood before or people-watching in the neighborhood you never visit. Listen to the podcast of your enemies and decide there is gold for you.

MAKING TOO MUCH

I come from the middle of Canada where we are experts in deflecting attention from ourselves. "Aw shucks, who me? It's an honor just to be here." In my hometown, I ate brunch at a cafe called The Tallest Poppy, likely a reference to the expression "The tallest poppy gets chopped down." The lesson to learn: it's dangerous to peek your head up over the status quo.

In the land of productivity, you must maintain just enough ambition to stay productive but not so much that you're a "bad" or "embarrassing" person. While you must not fall behind, you shouldn't make too many waves. You can make a life of marginal improvement, to keep up with inflation, and no more. You pay the most attention to the people just above and just below where you are and call them normal—the range of appropriate possibility.

On some level, as producers, we don't think we should *exist too much*. This turns into a habit of using our scruples against ourselves. Our concern for others "out there" (here we make sweeping gestures at a kind of person or collective problem) keeps us in line with what our shame at being human will allow.

"How dare you create when the world is on fire?" All your compassion, sensitivity, and imagination twists itself. "How dare you create [goodness, truth, beauty] when it doesn't fix all this?"

I say this with love: How dare you not. It is only your doing self that believes you are an outlier.

Beware of false humility. False humility will tell you to make sure you're "just right," all healed and free of rough edges before you can *really* show up. For everyone else's sake, of course. False humility will ask you to cross your arms at those who express freely and cannonball into the pool, then tell you to be smaller to protect yourself from those same judgments. (Ask me how I know.)

If I ask, "Who am I to make this meaningful action?" the satisfying answer will not be a list of justifications about my qualifications and worthiness, although that might be true enough. The real question is, Who do I think I am that needs so much protection?

Real humility is detaching from how important or unimportant, how good or not good, enough or not enough, you might be in order to surrender to the divine spark.

Making more life is not about being taller than the others, though you might stick out. Being willing to stick out, in the service of life, is humble.

Don't use the fact of evil, of war makers and legislators of injustice, as a reason not to create what was not there before. Do not reject the way your humanity throws off sparks of light because there is also darkness.

Truth and beauty are not frivolous. Creating is responsible, and responsibility is not grim. It is a gift to be alive. You do not serve the world with frantic action, but with your highest intelligence. You do not serve the world by withholding.

You might think of those who wish you would hold back. When you do something people don't expect, they often startle a little. Maybe your family will cooperate while also making a lot of grumbling noises as they do it. Maybe your friends will cheer you on or maybe they will act confused. Maybe everyone will immediately and graciously make room for you.

When you make a change in your life toward a fuller expression of your values, people can act a little weird. It's like you've just gone off script and their brains short-circuit trying to find a new line. Sometimes what comes out of their mouths is judgment, but they're really just trying to reconcile their old thoughts with reality.

Once I put on a reading series event in New York that made me nervous because I was interviewing an author I admired live in front of an audience. After grabbing a seat by the door, an acquaintance who was in the literary world said hello, cast a glance around the room, and sniffed. "Seems like everybody hosts a reading series these days."

Such noises and gestures from the back of the room have no inherent moral meaning. Other people's responses to your presence don't mean you shouldn't do something, and they don't mean you should. It's just how an ecosystem adjusts when new life is introduced.

That's the funny thing about creative living: it blows up the idea that more here means less over there. This is not a Take Time for You (thus Away from Other People, Because You're Worth It) self-care message. When you are more alive, there is just more life. Not less in others.

You are not burying your head in the sand. When you're done, your mind is less likely to spin or threaten you into frantic action. You can make clearer choices for others when you've chosen to create from love, not to mention the life you give to others through your efforts.

Making makes you come alive. Only in production land, which does not measure aliveness, could this be counted as a threat. Making what truly matters to you demands your loving attention. This is a skill, a way of being, that both you and the world require. When you create, you are practicing responding to what's in front of you with your highest intelligence. With all of you.

MAKING DELIGHT

You might believe you are running low on joy because you're taking your life too seriously. If only you could stop caring about the unanswered emails, dirty dishes, garden gathering weeds, the promotion that isn't yet yours, you would be content. You would even be accepting and loving, like the spiritual masters who float above the fray.

But you don't have to be careless about the to-dos; you can instead be more serious about delight.

Play is serious, so a maker takes play seriously. It is, after all, a primary feature of creation. The demands of this creation game require playing full out.

The first reason why: delight tends to dissolve our urge to control. It takes a cooperative approach toward reality. When you allow yourself to delight in something, you are open to being *charmed* by it. Unexpectedly and pleasantly transformed by it.

The more we practice delight, the more we are likely to notice our attempts to control that which is out of our control and none of our business, or defend something that does not need our defense (like our image, or an outworn idea of what *should be*). We are usually less kind, less collaborative, less imaginative, and frankly less effective without delight.

Of course, what feels delightful for me might be a pile of homework for you, and vice versa. I would prefer a root canal over a trip to Disneyland, but millions of others would disagree.

Yet delight doesn't live outside us in the right events or circumstances; it's a state of attention—and that can change.

Hasn't that happened to most of us "grown-ups"? Life turns gray so slowly we hardly notice; the same activity that *used* to be exciting and lively is now a drag. Why?

Because we lose touch with the sense of freedom we had when we started. We look at *who we are* differently within our relationship to our efforts: a Professional, a Person with Responsibilities, a Producer.

When this happens within our vocation—within the things we *chose* because they were supposed to be meaningful!—a quiet crisis descends. "I used to love this! Did I make a mistake? What do I need to fix? Am I lazy? Am I just being ungrateful or is this what adulthood is?" None of the above.

It's simply that the land of productivity frames delight as an occasional reward for real work but mostly as an indulgence for children and unserious people. Deep down, the land of productivity fears delight as a loss of control that must be monetized or marginalized.

Therefore, it doesn't even occur to most of us to solve for *delight*. And that's the first step—to practice it. In writing *The Book of Delights*, the poet and essayist Ross Gay discovered that "the more you study delight, the more delight there is to study."[1]

As you claim your birthright as a maker, you must become delightable. You must be willing to be charmed, to receive unexpected gifts and step out of a transactional relationship with reality. A producer will only see gifts as obligations and debts to be paid.

Delight is not a diversion. It is not a task you can fail to put on your to-do list; it is a part of your nature that will find its way into your life.

Here it is:

The milkweed your neighbor planted draws the butterflies to your sidewalk.

The way your grandmother calls it "The Walmart" and refuses to be corrected.

Your freshly washed sheets cool to the salt-lick touch of your skin on the muggiest night in August.

Even the behaviors that you might call bad habits, from the cat videos to the secret stash of potato chips in your cupboard, are delight elbowing its way into your day.

Your delight is already insisting on itself.

MAKING WITH CONFUSION

I came to expect the awkward silence when I asked my undergraduate students for their thoughts on the material. While I knew it was impossible for every one of them to have zero questions, concerns, or ideas, it was like pulling teeth to get them to share what they didn't understand. They had been taught that their role was to produce the right answers to get the grade to get the degree to get the job to get the money to get the stuff, and on it goes.

But outside the land of production, confusion is a highly creative state.

I know something good is growing when a maker confesses, "I don't know why, but . . ." Without fail, what falls out of their mouth afterward sounds like the truth.

"I don't know why, but I'm disappointed. Even though this is what I wanted."

"I don't know why, but this situation reminds me of my old boss."

Knowing *why* can mean an experience has already been categorized, its meaning stripped for parts. It's a butterfly in a frame.

Knowing *what to do* can simply mean "I've performed this role before. Nothing to learn here."

Confusion suggests that two seemingly conflicting ideas are on the table. Are you confused or are you being asked to accept two true things at once? Maybe they are mutually incompatible, maybe not. Maybe they are just both true, and a third truth is being born.

Are you confused or are you in the middle of a mystery that's still unfolding?

A maker discerns with more than the mind. As Blaise Pascal would have it, "The heart has its reasons, which reason does not know."[1]

MAKING HOPE DESPITE

This morning I danced to an exuberant pop-rap artist in my living room. At no point did I think, "This infectious song is bringing me life, but she really should have been solving climate change."

It goes without saying that we work to repair the world, and most of us have a visceral need to hope for a more beautiful future. But obsessive fault-finding attenuates this hope as it overwhelms you and keeps you (and this fault-finding *is* about you) inactive.

Your doing self brings up every ill in the world, every possible criticism, *every hard thing*, and says, "Yeah, but are you solving for *that*? If not, don't bother. Isn't it self-indulgent to share your inner world with the outer world?" In other words, "If I can't do everything, I will do nothing."

Over and over, makers tell me they are worried about the "self-indulgence" of their making. Why spend the time—an interesting financial metaphor—following the thread of my inner knowing? In *this* economy?

A writing teacher once told me that the purpose of writing a memoir was to show others the way your mind makes sense of life, and in doing so, the readers become more aware of their own consciousness.

As you sit across from a friend over coffee, don't you lean in as they share with you some dawning awareness, however untidy it is? When you are willing to be present with your inner knowing, to learn from it, and show the world what you've seen, you create hope.

Even the most nihilistic piece of expression is a contradiction—there's no such thing as making something that actually means nothing, if it's true.

It always means *you*. It means what you've learned about you. It means what you've learned about you and risked exposing to the world. It means who you are becoming.

What was the point of cave paintings? The experts don't yet agree. Ritual? Instruction? Storytelling? An offering to the gods? Yes, probably.

In the same way, no one agrees what poetry is for. Is it for the poet to feel themselves self-expressed? Or to tell someone you love them, but in a fancy way? Is it an art for edification of the sophisticated?

The question of use never ends, which is funny because it's a question that's trying to name what the "end" of these efforts is. What it's *for* will never find a satisfying answer.

All we can say for sure about the cave paintings is that they indicate a "who"—as in, there was a someone, somewhere, sometime who made this mark.

For a maker, it is not about the "why" but the "who." I am The Who that built this stone staircase in the hill. You are The Who I see clearly enough to bring food in the hospital. This is hope in a bottle.

What you make doesn't have to be "art," of course. It could be as simple as a conversation where you let your thoughts out into the air or a recipe for a three-layer cake. You share a Polaroid of your inner process as if to say, "Let me show you what I'm figuring out."

You are a maker in your very pores, and that means that you bring order where there was chaos. A mess of ideas, material, and images finds its place from your own rhyme and reason.

You make *sense* of things. You give us structures to feel, think, and act within.

Whether it's a meal for your partner or a haunting epic of everlasting genius, that's the nature of the process.

The idea that you contribute to the world like that might sound grandiose. But I say—with love and deep compassion for the overwhelm—the alternative is busy-ness masquerading as work.

Making is always an act of hope.

When I let go of my toddler's hands as she climbs up the slide, I hope she doesn't fall, but that's not the kind of hope I mean. It is not holding your breath and waiting for a positive result.

It is hope that a tiny part of life is worth attention. That's a profound assertion in the face of nihilism. To hope is to grasp between your fingers the thin string of life before you and follow it inch by inch, wherever it leads.

Keep going. Inch by inch is enough. We need what you can see from where you are.

MAKING WITH EVERYTHING YOU'VE GATHERED

As a producer, you have been taught to trust your conscious will first and foremost. That means that on the days where your motivation is weak, and your mind is full of doubts, on the days where you feel more goblin than human, you think you are deeply diminished.

As a maker, you must trust that you are more than your conscious will. This will unleash your creative capacities, since your power is no longer limited to the days where you *know* you can conquer the day.

Do not forget everything you are and everything you already know, all the golden nuggets of wisdom and hard-won skills that you have picked up through each year. It is easy to lose track since the productive world loves to break up every piece of life and separate them. But you are larger, more capable than a résumé can show.

You might have never sold your crafts before, but you have persuaded your friends to go see the movie you wanted to watch.

You might not have given a TED Talk, but you taught your brother how to tie his shoes as a kid and your friend everything you know about how to wood-fire a pizza.

You haven't appeared on a talk show, but you charmed the ornery cat next door. You know how to read the room.

In every "unproductive" period of your life, the divine spark within you has always been committed to your fullest expression, no matter where you ended up. You have found exactly what you needed where you were and brought it with you.

How much more of you could be present if you could trust that your knowing would unfold exactly at the right time? How much more would you show up if, instead of needing to have mastered all the moves for every unfamiliar or challenging circumstance, you knew that you were already that which is needed in the moment?

Trust how life has already prepared you instead of willing yourself to perform each day. Move from the mind to deep muscle memory. Your inner knowing is more nimble than your conscious mind anyway.

Even as the making path asks you to think like a beginner, it also asks you to trust your maturity so much that you don't need to be at 100 percent maximum shininess.

When you don't trust the tools sitting in your belt, you'll scramble for more and different. It keeps you consuming illusions of certainty, and very busy.

You may do this from the head and believe that your power, your mattering at all, will come from your excellence, certainty—your conscious confidence.

To rely on conscious confidence is a trap: not, as the land of productivity would say, because you have to do it anyway at all costs. But because it deems your sensitivity unsuitable; it calls your wobbly states of mind liabilities.

You will never know how much there is within you until you allow yourself to be seen making meaning, making your presence felt.

FOR NO REASON SEASON

In his book *The Institutes*, the fourth-century monk John Cassian tells a story about another, very curious fourth-century monk. His name was Abbot Paul, and he lived in the vast desert where he worshiped, prayed, and sustained himself. Date palms grew close to Abbot Paul, along with a small garden, so he never lacked for food. But, without needing to struggle for his material survival, he couldn't find any work to do.

He could make and sell his wares in town, but the cost of the trip through the desert for seven days would be more than he could make working. So, he set himself a task. He collected the leaves of the palms from the date trees and wove them into baskets and ropes, as if it were his job, "as if he was to be supported by it." He moved through the making for the way it focused his soul. And when a year had passed, and his cave was full of these woven palm leaves, he burned them all to dust and began again.[1]

You probably don't want to turn yourself into Abbot Paul: most of us couldn't anyway because we have to work to survive. The story is instead an allegory of what the labor process can do for us *in spite* of the survival imperative most of us have to work under.

When you labor to transform material around you and offer it back to the world—whether the result is remunerative or even useful—you also engage in *making*, in the sense I've been using that word. You reveal and expand your elemental qualities. You show yourself and others the way that you, and only you, can give effort, intention, purpose.

All we offer turns to dust in the end. Do not be precious. Make for who you become in the making.

The greatest trick the devil ever pulled was convincing us we needed reasons to try.

You have never needed a justification to wear your hair like Princess Leia, or call an old friend, or write a treatise against the overuse of beige in contemporary home design.

There are no gold stars or demerits that will grow your soul.

There will be no lawyers grilling you on the stand to explain why you wore graphic eyeliner, made a concept album about climate change, or wrote your novel at age seventy-eight.

We admit that some people will not get it, and we bless them, because every time we do it anyway, we make a little more space for them to meet us there.

We dare to leave it unexplained, even to ourselves. We let there be a gap of unknowing. We stop making so much sense.

We *do* have the time, because time will pass either way. We don't actually need our effort to go anywhere right now. Not yet. We welcome the absurd because it's delightful, compelling, or fun. As a by-product, we thumb our noses at the logic of scarcity and use, use, use.

We know this secret: our efforts will travel beyond us, because nothing true is wasted. Even when we are not yet sure why it's true or how it will nourish anything. In this way, our primary effort is trust, not strategy.

Declare it For No Reason Season.

BEGIN

When you get the inspiration, even the hint of an idea, this is a sacred moment. Do not rush to make big plans or set yourself a program you must fulfill. Remember that the desire to make something new, to extend yourself in any direction, means that you are already the person who can hold this idea and see it through.

Both the middle and the end will give you everything you need that you don't know you need yet. The how will reveal itself. You do not need to wait to become the person who can do it. You are already the one who does it.

Every time you start from where you are, you say yes to the fullness of your humanity now, not a hypothetical better version of you.

In production land, you thought you needed to get somewhere new to begin. Instead, begin with whatever is at hand.

How does nature begin its cycles of growth, decay, death, and rebirth? With reality. It rusts the wheelbarrow that's overturned and fills the empty birdbaths where the rain falls.

If you have forty-five minutes to make a meal, you start with what's in your cupboard. You don't start by searching for the best recipes of the century.

The urge to wait for perfection leads to more urgent waiting. The perfect moment is a myth, a horizon always fleeing as you approach. Make a pact with the minute you live in. Start from whatever your capacity holds, exactly as it is. Five minutes of brainstorming. One phone call. A walk around the block. Boredom is a place to start. Anger. Any sensation or observation. Once you can see what is, from your inner knowing, the maker in you is never without material.

MAKING BY ENDING ON PURPOSE

I met a young priest friend who just started a job serving a century-old parish on its last legs. The church's membership had dwindled to a dozen faithful people who filled two rows of pews every week in a building that could hold three hundred. These parishioners were locked in low-grade, decades-old squabbles that any visitor could sense. Finally, the bishop in charge decided this would be the church's last year before it merged with another congregation. He hired my priest friend to be its "death doula." This priest was excited. He leaned over the table to share his role like it was a secret. "I consider it an honor: I will help this version of the community have a good death."

"What does that mean?" I asked.

"It means dignity." He sat up straight in his chair. "We get to respect the last hundred years of this community's life together. And let go together. Without kicking and screaming."

As producers, we have one job: accumulating time, money, and energy. But a maker knows how to lose. A maker collaborates with life, after all, and that includes the part called decay.

We normally do a lot of work to avoid decomposition. When we know something is not working, the heart has stopped beating, we prefer to solve the problems that surround it, propping up the body like we're in *Weekend at Bernie's*.

Instead of having a hard conversation with our brother, we make extra plans so we'll miss that family gathering. Instead of staring blankly in response to a cruel joke, we fill in the silence with a note about the weather, then have five conversations on the side with everyone who was hurt. Instead of accepting that we don't like the role we're playing, we add minutes to our meditation practice to feel calm about it.

The following is an incomplete list of things that I've had to let decompose:

- My aspirational image of myself as a cool, mysterious person. That's not in the cards for me.
- My image of myself as a Good Person, which puts me constantly at risk of teetering off the tightrope into Badness.
- The esteem of people I wanted to impress at the cost of my inner knowing.
- Friendships with people who preferred when I was unhappy.
- A business model that was working but that my soul had outgrown.
- A novel that I will never write.
- My death-grip attachment to being right.

Letting go of these aspects of your life—the outdated self-images, the unsustainable relationships, the efforts whose time has come—isn't a defeat. It's an act of creative courage, an affirmation that you are more than the sum of your past decisions, more than the labels you've loved.

This isn't giving up; it's giving permission for life to grow, decay, and make itself new.

SUFFERING FROM CARING

My husband likes to tell the story of our second date and its aftermath. That day, we wandered around Brooklyn for seven hours, telling stories about our past and hinting about a shared future. After we parted ways, he called his best friend while lying down from dizziness. He explained that he did not know what to do with himself. As his head spun and his stomach flipped, his friend diagnosed the issue: "Yeah, that's what love feels like, bud."

There are many things that falling in love and living a creative life have in common, but one is frequently ignored: they can both find us disoriented, hiding under the covers.

What a dreadful passage we run through on the way to true desire. I'm reminded of how the etymology of "passion" means "suffering," or "that which must be endured." This is not to wallow in to prove how deep we are, nor is it a punishment we deserve for not becoming hedge fund managers. It's just the nature of undiluted wanting.

Passion reminds us that our control is limited and our heart extends outside our body. We've prepared, we've made all the moves we can, then all our best efforts have to leave our hands. Surrender is inevitable. We usually hate this.

Sometimes even anticipating the moment that the efforts you've made will leave your control is enough to stop you completely—just to avoid the sensation.

I used to find that so intolerable that I preferred the different suffering of only trying things I didn't care about that much. Or tweaking my efforts, making them a little safer, a little less intense, a little more strategic, and a little more beige.

You can do that, but you'll notice you feel less satisfied even if you "win," even if your efforts are well received. That's the way to suffer dispassionately. Tepid suffering. To me, that's worse.

Passion, and the sometimes vertiginous feeling of surrender it requires, is the price of admission for falling in love. Falling in love with a person or with something you create.

That feeling doesn't mean anything has gone wrong; quite the opposite. It doesn't mean you haven't prepared enough. You are not always supposed to feel like the Master of Your Domain, invulnerable to anything that happens, your heart protected with perfect strategy.

Yet like all sensation, it passes when you let it. Don't argue with your nervous system. Treat your body gently and give it a little time. Go under the covers for a while. Congratulate yourself for the willingness to love.

MAKING THE FUTURE

The philosopher Iris Murdoch calls us humans "creatures sunk in a reality whose nature we are constantly and overwhelmingly tempted to deform by fantasy."[1]

A fantasy is a story that you tell on top of what actually exists, that hides and protects you from yourself as you actually are and who you might become. In that way, a fantasy can never change us; it can only create more of the same. It can't nurture new life, it can only grow what is already overgrown.

Dreaming of colonizing Mars while the world burns is an exercise in fantasy because it applies resources and creative capacity to an ego problem that camouflages and leaves unchanged a real problem on the ground.

Billionaires will use this capacity to launch themselves into space with phallic rockets and to place their names on ever taller buildings, building castles for their egos into the sky. This use of the mind will never create more life or deeper flourishing; it will only demand resources.

As opposed to fantasy, imagination comes from seeing what it *is* so closely that you can't help discovering something new. This is how Copernicus found evidence that the earth orbits the sun: by studying the anomalies in planetary orbits so closely that the anomalies of the geocentric worldview outnumbered the evidence otherwise. He looked so closely at reality that a new possibility couldn't help but reveal itself.

You must have the courage to look so closely at the mundane and love it enough that it tells you what else is happening, that which was hidden by productive fantasy.

Imagination untangles and sees through fantasy.

To use your imagination is to take your reality so seriously, to get close to the irritation and impossible tensions in your life and look at them with wonder. Fantasy will rearrange the furniture and call it new.

Silicon Valley often specializes in producing solutions to problems that cannot touch the soul, by rearranging the shiny gadgets into new products, offering a remix of mundane conveniences: What if artificial intelligence could keep in touch with your siblings for you, or your fridge could order groceries? The next frontier: facial recognition for dog genealogy.

Your imaginative capacity will turn toward dissatisfaction with reality when it is not taken seriously. You will fantasize about a life with a wife who only argues with you "in a fun way" or a new car that stays gleaming. You have the capacity to make worlds in your mind, and this can be used for radical newness or static rearranging. As John Milton put it, "The mind is its own place and in itself can make a heaven of hell or a hell of heaven."[2]

You are the only one who can imagine from where your feet are planted today; this is not a job for the experts, or the lucky, because only you can see where you are clearly. You know what needs to change, to grow in your neighborhood, your corner of the internet, your office, your church, your pickleball team.

The future demands your imagination, your particular way of regenerating the earth. Without it, you are only going to tell the same stories that you were always told. You will only see the same things you've always seen, and only live to the same degree that you always have.

Living in your own fantasy is one thing. But when you don't actively use your imagination, you are just as likely to live in the fantasy of someone else, someone with more power, influence, and control.

You must free your imagination from the fantasies of people with bigger microphones, more confidence, and fewer obligations. They don't know what you know.

The world doesn't need more producers, who are so entangled in the fantasies of the powerful that they can only replicate exactly what's been done before. The nature of our life as makers is to use our imagination to see our way out of this, to see ourselves and the world as we actually are and could be.

It is easy to sit back and make wry observations about a world caught up in fantasy, to complain or thank your lucky stars that you're not like those unfortunate sheep in the system. But this only leads to its own form of atrophy and decay. Use your imagination to look at the real state of your own life, however unkempt or tangled it appears, cultivate it, and grow new things that will leave our future more whole.

MAKING A LEGACY

Very few of us will find our names in the record books, win a trophy for Best this or that, or see our faces carved in marble. Our legacies are wilder and more mysterious.

You are not meant to know how your efforts change people forever when you're not looking. The toddler in my home obsesses over the daffodils outside of one house on our block. Before my neighbor planted the bulbs, the child had never seen these bursts of yellow and white petals. Now she crouches down every day to remind herself of how they smell. Thanks to these plants and their loving gardeners, her senses have more to remember, yet my neighbors carry on with their errands with no idea. They cared just enough to place the bulbs in the ground, water, and pull weeds.

You aren't meant to know how your efforts matter. Trust that the impulse to plant, water, and weed is plenty. No checking notifications required. While you are sleeping, the beauty and wisdom you let flow through you when you were awake is finding its way to where it is needed.

I have never told my fourth-grade teacher that I remember walking away from her classroom for the last time as she called my name. Looking over my shoulder, I saw her standing in the doorframe, lit from behind by bright fluorescent lights. "Just don't forget to keep writing!" She waved. I've held the memory of the way she saw my eight-year-old dreams for thirty years.

Every look you share in the line for groceries, every minute you listen to a friend, every instance you choose sincerity over indifference, you etch a tiny, indelible mark on the universe. These marks are your true legacy, invisible and yet alive.

The beauty of this mysterious gift is that it's always unfolding, necessarily surprising. You can't plan it, you can't control it, and you certainly can't quantify it. And isn't that thrilling?

The sparks you made will fly long after you close your eyes for the last time. The core of your essence, the decisions you made, and the love you've scattered like seeds—all these feed the living ecosystem that generations yet unborn will call home. Your making time never ends.

As a maker, you let this change your calculations. What you craft is not confined to the limits of your mortality. No matter who does or doesn't notice it, your attention has transformed life into a timeless gift, nurturing truth, goodness, and beauty for this age and the world to come. Thank you for the offering. Thank you for being in your own process.

ACKNOWLEDGMENTS

I'm overwhelmed by the immense web of support and inspiration that held the creation of this book.

Nate, my partner in everything but crime—your brilliance and unwavering support have been the driving forces behind these words. Ingrid, my perpetual wellspring of inspiration—I will forever take notes on how to tackle life with your level of passion and life force.

To the dream team of coaches I got to work with throughout the writing process—Dr. Lauren Borden, Julie Flippen, Darla LeDoux, and Alana Schramm—your guidance has been invaluable, shaping not only the content of this book but also my growth as a person.

Stephanie Duncan Smith, my editor and wizard of words, your keen eye and kind guidance have transformed this collection of ideas into a coherent whole for readers to receive. Thanks for the editorial magic. To the whole Baker team—your efforts, often behind the scenes, have been crucial in orchestrating the myriad details that have brought this project to life. To my agent, Rachel Jacobson, thank you for your thoughtful advocacy and expertise navigating the intricate world of publishing.

To my family—Dad, Mom, my sisters Kate and Amy, and those I was lucky enough to inherit in marriage: Corby, Nick, and

Anna—thanks for being my constant support and loving ground to stand on.

To my teachers at the University of Minnesota, Yale Divinity School, and the Benedictine Peace Center—thanks for planting the seeds of thought that sprouted into this book.

A heartfelt thank-you to my clients—your stories and courage have been the heartbeat of this work. Your trust has been both an honor and a source of renewable energy for me.

To everyone else who played a role in this behind-the-scenes production (the fun kind of production), your fingerprints are all over this creation. Here's to you.

Love,
Maria

NOTES

Production Starts Now

1. Benedict of Nursia, *The Rule of St Benedict in English*, ed. Timothy Fry (Collegeville, MN: Liturgical Press, 1982) 7:26–29, 34. Emphasis mine.

2. Max Weber and Anthony Giddens, *The Protestant Ethic and the Spirit of Capitalism*, trans. Talcott Parsons (London: Routledge, 2001).

3. Frederick Taylor address at the dedication of the new engineering building of the University of Pennsylvania, October 19, 1906, in *Journal of the American Society of Mechanical Engineers*, 28 (1907): 924.

4. Frederick Winslow Taylor, *The Principles of Scientific Management* (New York: Harper and Brothers, 1919), 39.

5. Late in the writing process I was surprised to discover a very similar version of the story I'm telling about time in religion and workplace, with notable differences, in the work of Benjamin Snyder. It's a gift, and Snyder's excellent work shows the story is the truth. See Benjamin H. Snyder, *The Disrupted Workplace: Time and the Moral Order of Flexible Capitalism* (New York: Oxford University Press, 2016), 28.

6. Caitlin Rosenthal, *Accounting for Slavery: Masters and Management* (Cambridge: Harvard University Press, 2019), 200.

7. Rosenthal, *Accounting for Slavery*, 201.

8. Manufacturing giant Bethlehem Steel, for instance, fired Taylor when his efficiency reforms failed to have any effect on the company's bottom line. For the "all social activities" quote, see Taylor, *The Principles of Scientific Management*, 8.

9. E. Brooks Holifield, *God's Ambassadors: A History of the Christian Clergy in America* (Grand Rapids: Eerdmans, 2007), 160.

10. C. Wright Mills, *White Collar: The American Middle Classes* (Oxford: Oxford University Press, 1951), xvii.

11. Shoshana Zuboff, "The White-Collar Body in History," in James Cortada, ed., *The Rise of the Knowledge Worker* (Boston: Butterworth-Heinemann, 2009), 217.

12. Peter Drucker, *The Practice of Management* (Oxford: Elsevier, 1954).

13. Luc Boltanski and Eve Chiapello, *The New Spirit of Capitalism* (London: Verso, 2005), 76.

14. In Bill Price and David Jaffe, *The Frictionless Organization* (Oakland: Berrett-Koehler Publishers, 2022), 251.

The Other Path

1. Agnes de Mille, *Martha: The Life and Work of Martha Graham* (New York: Vintage Books, 1991), 264.

Mere Doing

1. Friedrich Nietzsche, "Schopenhauer as Educator," *Untimely Meditations*, trans. R. J. Hollingdale (Cambridge: Cambridge University Press, 1983), 158.

2. Hannah Arendt, *The Human Condition* (Chicago: University of Chicago Press, 1958), 137.

Doing Enough

1. Edward Brooke-Hitching, *The Phantom Atlas: The Greatest Myths, Lies and Blunders on Maps* (San Francisco: Chronicle Books, 2018), 73.

2. Donald MacMillan, *Four Years in the White North* (New York and London: Harper and Brothers, 1918), 80.

3. Mary Morton Cowan, *Captain Mac: The Life of Donald Baxter MacMillan, Arctic Explorer* (Honesdale, PA: Calkins Creek, 2010), 70.

Doing Middle Management

1. Richard Schwartz, PhD, *No Bad Parts: Healing Trauma and Restoring Wholeness with the Internal Family Systems Model* (Boulder, CO: Sounds True, 2021), 7.

2. Pablo Neruda, "We Are Many," trans. Alastair Reid, in William Sieghart, ed., *The Poetry Remedy: Prescriptions for the Heart, Mind, and Soul* (New York: Viking, 2019), 77.

Doing Free Time

1. Heraclitus, *Fragments*, trans. Brooks Haxton (New York: Penguin, 2003), 81.

Doing Deep Effort

1. Thomas Benner Smith, *If It Is to Be, It's Up to Me: How to Develop the Attitude of a Winner and Become a Leader* (Hummerlstown, PA: Possibility Press, 2001).

2. Geoffrey Chaucer, *The Complete Works of Geoffrey Chaucer*, vol. 4, ed. Walter W. Skeat (Oxford: Clarendon Press, 1894), 579.

3. John Lydgate, *Lydgate's Troy Book: AD 1412–20*, ed. Frederick James Furnivall (Cambridge: Harvard University Press, 1906), 1730.

Dread and Doing

1. William M. Bowsky, *The Black Death: A Turning Point in History?* (New York: Holt, Rinehart and Winston, 1971), 14.
2. William K. Klingaman and Nicholas P. Klingaman, *The Year Without Summer: 1816 and the Volcano That Darkened the World and Changed History* (New York: St. Martin's Press, 2013), 118.
3. Mark Fisher, *Capitalist Realism: Is There No Alternative?* (Ropley, UK: O Books, 2009), 1.

Procrastination

1. Daphne K. Lee in Shelby Deering, "How to Break the Cycle of Revenge Bedtime Procrastination and Get Yourself to Sleep," *Real Simple*, September 19, 2023, www.realsimple.com/revenge-bedtime-procrastination-7560701#:~:text =In%202020%2C%20journalist%20Daphne%20K,freedom%20during%20late%20night%20hours.

Efficiency

1. William J. Donovan, *Simple Sabotage Field Manual* (Washington, DC: Office of Strategic Services, 1944), 30.

Undoing Fixing

1. Sheila Heti, *How Should a Person Be?* (Toronto: House of Anansi Press, 2010), 15.

Undoing Punishment

1. Herman Melville, *The Piazza Tales and Other Prose Pieces* (Evanston and Chicago: Northwestern University Press, 1987), 23.

Undoing Discipline

1. Oliver Stoll, "The Religions of the Armies," in *A Companion to the Roman Army*, ed. Paul Erdkamp (Oxford: Blackwell Publishing, 2007), 453.

Undoing Sentimentality

1. Ann and Barry Ulanov, *Primary Speech* (Louisville: Westminster John Knox Press, 1982), 1.

Perhaps

1. Samuel Beckett, *Endgame and Act Without Words* (New York: Grove Press, 2009), 70.

Numbness

1. Audre Lorde, *Sister Outsider: Essays and Speeches* (Berkeley: Crossing Press, 2007), 131.

Undoing Imposter Syndrome

1. Henri Nouwen, *The Wounded Healer* (New York: Doubleday, 2013), 93.

Boredom

1. Simone Weil, *The Need for Roots* (London: Routledge, 2020), 32.

Inventing Creativity

1. Marc Andreesen, "The Techno-Optimist Manifesto," October 16, 2023, https://a16z.com/the-techno-optimist-manifesto/.
2. William Wordsworth, preface to *Lyrical Ballads*, 1802 edition, in *The Complete Poetical Works of William Wordsworth*, vol. 10 (New York: Cosimo Inc., 2010), 18.
3. Matthew Arnold, "The Function of Criticism," in *"Culture and Anarchy" and Other Writings*, ed. Stefan Collini (Cambridge: Cambridge University Press, 1993), 28.
4. Boltanski and Chiapello, *The New Spirit of Capitalism*, 75.

A Burning Spark

1. Gospel of Thomas v. 70 in James McConkey Robinson, ed., *The Nag Hammadi Library in English* (Leiden: E. J. Brill, 1984), 126.

Making Intimacy

1. Robin Wall Kimmerer, *Braiding Sweetgrass: Indigenous Wisdom, Scientific Knowledge, and the Teachings of Plants* (Minneapolis: Milkweed Editions, 2013), 252.

It's Not About You

1. Karen Jensen, "The Significance and Pedagogic Applications of the Vocal Breakthrough. Part II: The Role of Attention," *Journal of Singing* 72, no. 3 (January/February 2016): 355–361.

Making with Gurus and Enemies

1. Walt Whitman and Francis Murphy, *Walt Whitman: The Complete Poems* (London: Penguin, 2004), 37.
2. This and subsequent Reed quotes in this chapter are from Ishmael Reed, *19 Necromancers from Now* (Garden City, NY: Doubleday, 1970), 22.

Making Delight

1. Ross Gay, *The Book of Delights: Essays* (Chapel Hill, NC: Algonquin Books, 2019), 39.

Making with Confusion

1. Blaise Pascal, *Pascal's Pensées* (New York: E. P. Dutton & Co., 1958), 78.

For No Reason Season

1. John Cassian, *Institutes*, 10.26.

Making the Future

1. Iris Murdoch, "Against Dryness: A Polemical Sketch," *Encounter* 16 (January 1961): 16–20.
2. John Milton, *Paradise Lost*, book 1, lines 254–55.

MARIA BOWLER is a writer, coach, and retreat leader. She holds a masters in religion and the arts from Yale University, is a former magazine editor, and has taught creative writing at the university level. Canadian by birth, she now lives in the Driftless region of the US with her family.

Connect with Maria:

www.MariaBowler.com

 @MariaEVBowler

 MariaBowler.substack.com